PRAISE FOR *THE E*

In his wonderfully down-to-earth, transparent style, Steve Cuss has given us another gift in *The Expectation Gap*. This is the most helpful book I've read in my thirty-five years of ministry when it comes to recognizing, naming, and bridging the gap between what we believe about God and what we experience from God. Steve has given us practical tools to identify deeply held patterns, beliefs, and habits that hold us back from truly encountering God, inspiring us to do the work so we can experience the fullness of love, joy, and peace that is ours in Christ.

CHRISTINE CAINE, founder of A21 and Propel Women

If you've ever felt like there's more to explore in your relationship with God, you're probably correct. In these pages, Steve Cuss, a trusted guide for many leaders, reveals the missing pieces you've been searching for.

CAREY NIEUWHOF, bestselling author of *At Your Best*, podcaster, and founder of the Art of Leadership Academy

Steve Cuss's new book is a welcome addition to the literature that applies systems theory to everyday life and growth. I found myself laughing and being pierced with truth—all at the same time as I read this fresh, practical, and playful book. If you seek to understand these important concepts while using the tools Steve offers, I have no doubt you will experience growth, transformation, and a new freedom you may have never thought possible.

RUTH HALEY BARTON, author of *Strengthening the Soul of Your Leadership* and founder of Transforming Center

Steve Cuss has a remarkable ability to meet us right where we're stuck and point the way to freedom. *The Expectation Gap* will be immensely helpful for anyone longing to experience God more fully and seeking to become aware of major obstacles along the path.

CHUCK DEGROAT, author of *When Narcissism Comes to Church*, and professor of pastoral care at Western Theological Seminary, Holland, Michigan

Steve Cuss is a reliable guide and a trustworthy friend who has helped me navigate the relational dynamics of life and leadership. Now he takes the conversation to the deepest level by focusing on our relationship with God and its connection to our relationship with ourselves and with others. By means of astute diagnostics and precise tools, Cuss helps us name and close the gaps in our experience of God. The result is a beautiful journey to the heart's true home—the presence of a loving God.

GLENN PACKIAM, lead pastor, Rockharbor Church, and author of *The Resilient Pastor* and *The Intentional Year*

Steve Cuss extends a hand to those of us navigating the sometimes-bewildering journey of faith, where the realities of God's presence and love often seem distant. Through his candid sharing of personal struggles and the breakthroughs that transformed his pastoral ministry, Steve offers not just empathy but practical tools to bridge the gap between our intellectual beliefs and our heart's experience. His insights challenge the often-unspoken norms within our faith communities, encouraging a journey toward a more authentic, tangible relationship with God. As a fellow traveler on this journey, I believe *The Expectation Gap* will be a beacon of hope for many, illuminating a path to experiencing the peace, freedom, and love promised in Christ.

TARA BETH LEACH, pastor and author of *Emboldened*

We wouldn't be exaggerating to say that no author has shaped our leadership more than Steve Cuss in the last several years. Steve is speaking to a fundamental challenge that most Christians face but are rarely honest about—the distance between what we profess to be true about God and our actual experience of those truths. With his trademark, straight-to-the point clarity, he illuminates hidden dynamics that stunt our personal growth, which is why we regularly tell our friends, family, and peers, "If you aren't reading Steve Cuss, you should be."

IKE AND SHARON MILLER, PhDs, authors and pastors of Bright City Church in Durham, North Carolina

Too often our daily experience doesn't live up to the miraculous, life-changing, world-shaking faith we see in Scripture, and so we feel far from God. Steve Cuss reveals how our experience of God can be derailed by our own baggage, narratives, and expectations and offers honest, practical tools to imagine the possibility that God has gone nowhere. Thank you, Steve, for helping us get out of our own way . . . and God's.

MANDY SMITH, pastor and author of *The Vulnerable Pastor*

For many Christians, the difference between their personal beliefs about God, themselves, and the world, and their lived experiences is a chasm difficult to face, but Steve Cuss is the gentle and affirming voice that speaks to the unhealthy expectations that rise out of our culture, communities, and preconceived ideas about the way we think things should be. He doesn't seek to fill the gap, but instead honors and nurtures it so we can see that it is not the God of our beliefs who has failed us. It is the thing we have not yet noticed—that God is standing on the precipice with us and staring down that same abyss.

PHUC LUU, PhD, author of *Jesus of the East*

Most of us were taught somewhere along the way the idea that Christianity is not a religion, but a relationship. But what if my relationship with God has not turned out the way I expected? John Calvin taught that all "true and sound wisdom" comes at the intersection of "the knowledge of God and the knowledge of self." The *Expectation Gap* helps us understand how to grow in this true wisdom. Steve compellingly challenges clichés about God and relationships and what it means to be in a growing relationship with God. If you're open to taking an honest look at yourself, this book will surely encourage you.

TOD BOLSINGER, cofounder and principal of AE Sloan Leadership and author of *Tempered Resilience*

The Expectation Gap is a must-read for anyone who has a desire to deepen their connection to God. Steve has been a close friend for more than fifteen years, and his spiritual journey has been inspiring and encouraging for me. I have often struggled to reconcile my own experiences with my expectations of God. Steve's teachings have gotten me get unstuck and moving in a new and exciting direction. This book is an antidote for spiritual drift, and I'm confident it will help you experience God in new and fresh ways.

DAVE RUNYON, coauthor of *The Art of Neighboring*

It has been my great privilege to work closely with Steve Cuss for more than a decade now. I've watched him expand, refine, and clarify these tools into a way of life that can be grasped and implemented by anyone who wants to be well. His humor, boldness, and faith in Jesus make him an excellent guide on the journey to experience God more often in our daily lives. This book represents his best thinking to date and is a wonderful invitation to encounter the goodness of God more fully.

JIMMY CARNES, coach with Capable Life and Steve's colleague

In *The Expectation Gap*, my friend, pastor, coworker, and mentor Steve Cuss helps us poke at some nagging questions about faith. Steve provides a revolutionary framework to think through our own expectations of God—and his insights do not disappoint. He applies the elements of family systems theory—by asking inquisitive questions and identifying stuck patterns—to shed light on these gaps. He also provides practical insight into human-sized practices we can use to bridge them. This is accessible theology for an accessible God. Through these pages we see the gospel again as God intended—as good news!

TOM MORRIS, elder and friend of Steve

An absolute necessity for your transformational tool box. With wit and wisdom forged through his own life and workplace experience, Steve Cuss offers true power tools that move far beyond information and deliver on the change we all long for. Combined with the grace of the Spirit of God and the courage to apply the teaching, Steve's teaching will ease you into the goodness of the gifts God offers, and the gap between what you know and what you feel about God's love will seem much smaller as change comes.

LINNEA SPICER, elder and Steve's colleague

Steve takes readers into a deeper understanding of how chronic anxiety infects our discernment and experience of God's deep and abiding love. He doesn't leave us with just a better understanding, but instead asks provocative questions and provides concrete tools to explore the gap between our theological beliefs and experiences of God. Join the journey toward relaxing into the presence of God as the beloved.

RENAE LORING, pastor, spiritual director, and Steve's colleague

THE EXPECTATION GAP

THE EXPECTATION GAP

The Tiny, Vast Space between Our Beliefs and Experience of God

STEVE CUSS

ZONDERVAN REFLECTIVE

The Expectation Gap

Published in Grand Rapids, Michigan, by Zondervan. Zondervan is a registered trademark of The Zondervan Corporation, L.L.C., a wholly owned subsidiary of HarperCollins Christian Publishing, Inc.

Requests for information should be addressed to customercare@harpercollins.com.

Zondervan titles may be purchased in bulk for educational, business, fundraising, or sales promotional use. For information, please email SpecialMarkets@Zondervan.com.

ISBN 978-0-310-15706-9 (audio)

Library of Congress Cataloging-in-Publication Data

Names: Cuss, Steve, 1971- author.
Title: The expectation gap : the tiny, vast space between our beliefs and experience of God / Steve Cuss.
Description: Grand Rapids, Michigan : Zondervan Reflective, [2024] | Includes bibliographical references.
Identifiers: LCCN 2023051519 (print) | LCCN 2023051520 (ebook) | ISBN 9780310156376 (softcover) | ISBN 9780310156390 (ebook)
Subjects: LCSH: Presence of God. | God (Christianity)—Omnipresence. | Christian life. | BISAC: RELIGION / Christian Living / Spiritual Growth RELIGION / Spirituality
Classification: LCC BT180.P6 C87 2024 (print) | LCC BT180.P6 (ebook) | DDC 231.7—dc23/eng/20240129
LC record available at https://lccn.loc.gov/2023051519
LC ebook record available at https://lccn.loc.gov/2023051520

Published in association with the literary agency of Pape Commons, Colorado Springs, CO.

Cover design: Derek Thornton / Notch Design
Cover photo: © Dragan Milovanovic / Shutterstock
Interior design: Sara Colley

Printed in the United States of America

24 25 26 27 28 LBC 6 5 4 3 2

To my mum,
who passed away during the writing of this book.
Your resilience and capacity astonished me.
I marveled at your bravery to learn new things.
I will forever remember and enjoy your quick and wicked wit.

To those who deeply believe
but get stuck in their faith,
and to those who want to believe
but can't find the evidence or experience of God.
I remain convinced
that the very heartbeat of the universe is love,
and his name is Jesus.
I hope this book helps you encounter
the freedom, peace, and love of God.

CONTENTS

INTRODUCTION

GAPS AND TRAPS

Your new life is going to cost you your old one.
BRIANNA WIEST, *THE MOUNTAIN IS YOU*

Many of us struggle with a gap between what we believe about God and what we experience from God. We believe things about God that we actually struggle to encounter in our daily lives. Sometimes our best efforts to mind these gaps keep us stuck and spinning—lots of energy, not much progress. Some of us are honest about the struggle; some speak or act as though they have no gaps; only a very few don't experience a gap at all.

I think the keenest gaps are these:

1. I believe God loves me, but I don't feel it.
2. I believe God is with me, but I don't see him.
3. I thought I'd be further along by now.

Three gaps—God's particular love, God's visceral presence, and my spiritual progress.

I want to help us mind these gaps so that what we believe will be more congruent with our experience. We will always have gaps, of course, but I believe we can find a way to approach them in a soul-satisfying way. How do we mind these gaps? How do we live so that our cognitive beliefs infect and infuse the deepest parts of ourselves? We don't want our faith to be merely conceptual; we want to experience it viscerally. We believe in the peace and freedom of Christ, but we often struggle to embody our beliefs.

Ask yourself this: Do you truly experience the benefits Jesus said you would get when you follow him? Jesus and the writers of the New Testament promised that the outcome of following Jesus would be peace, freedom, and love, but if we were to take an honest inventory of our lives, most of us would have to admit we do not live in those realities on a daily basis. We are often frazzled, hurried, and bound. We get too easily stuck in the same patterns. We carry levels of shame and condemnation that can be discouraging at best and debilitating at worst. We believe in our heads, but we have trouble letting our cognitive beliefs seep into the deeper parts of ourselves. My hope is to help each of us embody freedom and live in the peace and love that God has for us so we can relax into the presence of God.

We find ourselves in a conundrum. We have oriented our whole existence around a set of beliefs we struggle to absorb and a set of outcomes that elude us much of the time.

I'm not saying Jesus guaranteed an easy or comfortable life. Jesus offers peace, freedom, and love, but he also promises suffering, persecution, and death. The paradox of the Christian faith, or perhaps the wonder of it, is that we can experience peace, freedom, and love in the midst of suffering, persecution, and death. These promises are not mutually exclusive. Naturally, we want God to remove our difficult circumstances, but instead God infects them (in a good way!). God comes right into our mess and abides with us so that our circumstances do not hinder our freedom. So, yes, a life with Christ can include great suffering and pain. But it is also true that God's peace, freedom, and love are more elusive to us than they ought to be.

The good news is, we don't actually need this experience all the time to have a breakthrough. I have found that if I can encounter God's peace, freedom and love even 10 or 15 percent of the day, it can be transformative. So I am not proposing some form of utopian existence where we bask in the reality of God's love all the time. I'm just suggesting we could all use a taste of it more often—a foretaste, a preview of the banquet that is to come. An appetizer will get us by just fine until the main course comes. When these fundamentals of our faith elude us most of the time, we can't help but wonder if the main course is ever coming.

In the Lord's Prayer, Jesus taught us to pray, "Your kingdom come, your will be done, on earth as it is in heaven" (Matthew 6:10). When I read this prayer, my tendency is to think of earth as "the world out there." But how often do we neglect our own little piece of real estate right here in our bodies? "Your kingdom come on earth"—yes—but also "your kingdom come in earth." You and I are made of earth, and God is equally establishing his kingdom reign within us as well as around us. But for many followers, we focus exclusively on the broken places around us. What would this world be like if we were to focus more on God's reign—God's peace and freedom first seeping into the depths of our interior world?

We crave to feel alive with the presence and love of God more often. It is a struggle, isn't it?

In *Aurora Leigh*, Elizabeth Barrett Browning wrote:

> Earth's crammed with heaven,
> And every common bush afire with God:
> But only he who sees, takes off his shoes,
> The rest sit round it, and pluck blackberries.[1]

Barrett Browning beautifully suggests that we can see God all around us if we just know how to look. I would simply add that I have,

---

1. Elizabeth Barrett Browning, *Aurora Leigh* (New York: C. S. Francis, 1857), 275–76.

on rare occasion, warmed my naked toes by a shrub aflame with God. But it's also true that I forage for blackberries. I have eaten 1.67 tons of blackberries in my pursuit of God's tangible presence. That number is an estimate, most assuredly rounded down.

I am a pastor who has grappled with these gaps for most of my adult life. For years I struggled to experience God's specific love for me in a visceral, soul-satisfying way. I had no trouble believing that God loves people, and I especially had no trouble believing that God loves you, dear reader. But experiencing God's particular love eluded me. I have gone long stretches of time without a genuine awareness of God's presence. My faith tradition is heavily cognitive, and my own personality is bent that way, so by default I lack awareness of God's presence. When I am faced with a problem, my first inclination is not to seek God but to figure it out for myself. My brain's default postures are *think harder* and *worry your way to peace.* This approach is not conducive to minding the expectation gap. I needed to find another way of being, but I wasn't sure how to go about it.

In 2016, I had a breakthrough. Until then, my life had been inching toward an unsatisfying theology I couldn't shake. I very much believed in God and spent my life serving God, but I found that my daily experiences with God were markedly different from my cognitive beliefs about God. My spiritual practices would sometimes make a dent in the gap between my belief and experience, but my default was toward practicing a form of deism. I knew cognitively that God was not distant and uninvolved, but my daily experience indicated otherwise.

I was a well-meaning hypocrite, helping others experience a faith I was struggling to experience myself. I loved pastoring and saw it as the great privilege of my life, but I considered resigning. It wasn't due to some scandal or fear of exposure. I wasn't hiding anything from my congregation or my elder board. On the contrary, I have always been honest with my congregation about my own faith, sharing about my doubt and my struggles to encounter God's love. I believe frank honesty from a pastor is a gift to congregants who don't know what to do with their own quiet struggles. If I as a pastor bring my challenges out into the open, it gives congregants permission to share theirs as well.

I had led and preached from that posture for years. Still, I wondered if I could keep going, proclaiming a gospel I had oriented my whole life around and believed in my brain and yet struggled to experience. I wondered if my congregation needed a pastor who could more easily access God. Honestly, I wondered if pastoring was the problem. Maybe working for God was blocking my capacity to encounter God.

That statement might surprise you, but it probably does not surprise the pastors reading this. Often, church leaders are too much God's employees and not enough God's children. We tend to focus on others to the neglect of our own well-being. Many people of faith are like that too. We like to help others, but we don't like to be helped. We pour out, out, out and become confused when our own well is dry.

My 2016 breakthrough turned out to be simple. The problem was a set of deeper habits, beliefs, and patterns I held—and that had hold of me. They were a series of harmful expectations—internal and external—that were blocking my capacity to engage God.

DEEPEST VERSUS MOST PRECIOUS BELIEFS

I always assumed my belief in God was my deepest core belief. I converted to Christianity from an agnostic upbringing. Jesus completely revolutionized my life, and I thought I was giving all to him. I relocated to a new country to pursue the best theological education I could afford, and it has been the privilege of my life to serve God as a pastor. I try to sift all my decisions, actions, and attitudes through the person and teaching of Jesus as my sovereign Lord and King. How, then, could my belief in Jesus not be my deepest core belief?

As I studied the gaps in my faith and explored why I was struggling to encounter peace, freedom, and love, I discovered that I hold beliefs even deeper and more foundational to me than my belief in Jesus.

This was alarming at first, but it proved beneficial to locate those underlying beliefs and bring them to the surface for serious examination. Some of those beliefs are subconscious, some run on autopilot, and most of them are based on assumptions I hold about myself and about God that are not true. I think it will also help you to consider that you hold beliefs that are deeper than your belief in God—beliefs that may be blocking your connection with God.

Think of it this way: A precious belief is one we hold dearly; a deepest belief is one that holds us, which is why such a belief can be harder to locate. It holds us back. It blocks our capacity to experience our most precious belief. Another way to look at it is to examine "head" beliefs and "body" beliefs. My head holds my precious belief in God, but my body reacts to beliefs that have taken hold of me. I can often locate my deepest beliefs when I am under pressure or when things don't go my way. I suddenly feel like everything is on my shoulders, that I need to do something to change course or figure out what is going on. I forget that God is with me and instead depend completely on myself.

Some of my deepest core beliefs run on autopilot. I don't remember choosing them, but they take charge regularly. A simple example relates to God's love. I say I believe God loves me, but my deeper belief operates as if I am not worth loving. My precious belief says God loves me particularly and specifically, that God is involved in my life. Yet my deepest core belief says that God loves me generically and that I have to sort things out for myself. Uncovering core beliefs can take time, but you might take a few moments now to begin reflecting on your own core beliefs.

A SOLUTION OUTSIDE OF THE "FAITHY" THINGS

For years, I had been applying the wrong solution. The actual solution came from a surprising source. I had assumed the tools to help me deepen my experience of God were limited to what I call "faithy" things—tools like prayer, Scripture, and community. Instead, the solution came from a different source. Many of my readers are huge fans of those faithy things, so before you quickly put the book down, let me get this out of the way now. The problem was not the faithy things, but rather my *approach* to them. I was applying the more-of-the-same and try-harder mentality to things that were not necessarily working. Many of us get stuck in this cycle. Something isn't working, but the more-of the-same and try-harder methods are all we know to do. And so we stay stuck and spinning. I had to step out of that cycle to learn a different approach so I could go back to the faithy things in a different way.

The solution to this expectation gap surprised and embarrassed me because it was something I had known for twenty years. In the next chapter, I will introduce you to this solution and the tools it led me to adopt, but for now I'll simply say that, earlier in my life, I learned a transformative approach to my own well-being and to cultivating healthy relationships in the workplace and at home. I've used this approach in my leadership, pastoring, marriage, parenting, and friendships for twenty years. In short, this theory helps us notice the dynamics that affect every precious relationship we have. It helps us pay attention to assumptions and manage triggers both in ourselves and in our relationships with other people. When we dive deeper into this theory, we learn how to identify recurring stuck patterns in our relationships.

I first learned this theory in the intense world of trauma and hospice chaplaincy, where death, serious sickness, and tragedy were nonstop realities. It didn't take long for that intense crucible to expose triggers, assumptions, and family dynamics that had influenced me—things I didn't even know I had. My job was to help people through the worst moments of their lives, but I was surprised to discover how much of that job was about managing myself so I could be fully present to them in their pain. I never imagined all that was underneath the surface of my awareness that could get in the way of my being connected, aware, and present to others in tragic times.

After being taught this theory as a chaplain, I studied it in graduate school and slowly forged a set of emotional and relational health tools that have served me well in the decades since. I've been teaching these tools to leaders for years now, helping them notice and manage their own dynamics so they can be more present to others. These tools form the basis of my first book, *Managing Leadership Anxiety: Yours and Theirs*.[2] But I'm embarrassed to admit that it took until 2016 to realize that I had been studying, practicing, and teaching a set of tools to help people navigate their precious relationships but hadn't thought to apply them to my most precious relationship—my relationship with God.

D'oh.

It revolutionized my faith. Seriously. In this book, I will introduce you to these tools so you can apply them too. Of course, I still have an expectation gap. I still have times when I am not aware of God or do not experience God's love. I still grapple with God's perceived silence, and I find God's "still small voice" (1 Kings 19:12 KJV) to be difficult. I am not some mystical faith guru. There is no Yoda in me. I am still an "earthen vessel" (2 Corinthians 4:7 KJV), seeking a foretaste of heaven like you are. But I am no longer stuck, and I no longer live in a low-grade condemnation of shame. I have learned to allow God's voice of love to sneak past my own defense mechanisms. I am comfortable being vulnerable and exposed in God's presence—without pretense or performance. I now know what God's freedom feels like in my body. I can relax into God's presence, even in the middle of massive challenges.

Anyone can do this. It is not difficult work, but it is brave work. You do not have to be smart; you just have to be intentional,

---

2. Steve Cuss, *Managing Leadership Anxiety: Yours and Theirs* (Nashville: Thomas Nelson, 2019).

courageous, and patient. I am able to do this between 10 and 30 percent of the time in my life. We all want Utopia, and many of us want a 100 percent grade on everything we do, but I've discovered that even encountering God in these ways just a few times a day or a week can be utterly transformative. And this is good news if you decide to try some of these tools for yourself. An early win can encourage you to keep going.

HOW TO READ THIS BOOK

The chapters in this book are a series of pairs. In each pair, there is an introductory chapter that describes a particularly common and irritating gap between our beliefs and our experience of God. The second chapter in the pair offers tools and additional insights for applying the ideas from the previous chapter. Some of the tools may serve you better than others. You can pick and choose whatever works best as you go through the book. I believe these tools can help you get unstuck and experience freedom in real time.

You can read this book alone and begin to put these tools into practice, but you will benefit exponentially more by processing the insights in community. Our deepest beliefs, fears, shame, and hopes all make us feel quite vulnerable, so they tend to keep us isolated and stuck. In this book, we will discover that the heart of our work is listening to and challenging assumptions, and there is no replacement for a community that helps us speak against the isolating voice of our inner critic, our raging perfectionism, or the other parts of our lives that keep us stuck and bound. I recommend finding a trustworthy community where you can share, discuss, listen, and encourage one another. You will get much further together than alone.

Also, a quick word to any of you who will lead group discussions. You will be most helpful to your people if you can create a safe space for them to be exactly themselves. Take the extra step of managing your own desire to advise or fix; at the same time, graciously steer others in the group away from trying to teach, correct, or fix. Christian community can tend toward the pressure to make something better or put a neat bow on complex situations. The work we are doing in this book is slow and vulnerable, and some of your folks may be working things out in real time, for the first time in their lives after decades of being and behaving another way. As a group leader, you can focus as much on context in the group as you do on content. If people can share honestly, which means they may share imperfectly, and you can welcome it, you will all have a rich experience.

I hope this approach can bring you some relief and clarity, regardless of what brings you to this book. Many followers of Jesus these days carry much anxiety, pain, or even church trauma and are struggling to connect to God. I have prayed over and over as I wrote this—that you will experience healing and a breakthrough. I should warn you that the fight for freedom takes courage and tenacity, but it is worth it. I have a few battle scars from my own journey.

If you study freedom movements throughout history, a common thread emerges. The oppressors never willingly hand over power to the oppressed. Moses fought Pharaoh; Martin Luther King Jr. fought oppressive systems. They had to fight for their freedom. There is much underneath the surface in our own lives that keeps us oppressed and pushed down. It might be a battle to escape all of those complicated dynamics. But be of good hope! We do not fight this battle alone. God is with us. God has been inviting us all along into freedom, peace, and love.

Let's go, shall we?

ONE

OUR FALSE REALITY

There's only one place that God doesn't dwell in—illusion. God only abides in truth.

RICH VILLODAS, TWITTER

Have you ever felt like you were on a treadmill to nowhere? It is difficult to get off a treadmill like that, but it's almost impossible when you don't know you're on a treadmill in the first place. So much of our faith experience is deeply tied to our assumptions about ourselves—the false reality we live in. We don't stop to think about these assumptions; they just sort of keep us running, wearing us down. And they play a critical role in creating and maintaining the gaps between our expectations and experience of God.

We will treat each gap specifically in upcoming chapters, but before we do, we need to focus on two pressing matters that provide the foundation for this whole way of being. The first matter: make an intentional shift in your approach to two core relationships. If you make one simple shift in each of these relationships, your capacity to experience God will expand.

The second matter is harder but equally important: learn the four most common dynamics that infect every relationship and notice how they hinder your daily experience of God. When people seek professional counseling, the counselor is often listening for these dynamics because every counselor knows they are the most common dynamics that damage relationships.

The four dynamics are tricky because we all experience them but somehow struggle to notice them. When you read about them below, several examples will likely come to mind in your own relationships. But then tomorrow, chances are you'll get wrapped up in them before you know it. While we may catch these dynamics intuitively, if we can learn to notice them some of the time instead of getting caught up in them, the quality of our relationships can experience massive improvements.

There is no need to bury the lede here. These same dynamics infect our relationship with God as well. That's right, the same dynamics that infect our friendships, marriages, and families also impact our relationship with God.

These two shifts and four dynamics will help increase our capacity for *connectedness* and also increase our awareness of when we are *disconnected*. Connectedness is quite simply the cornerstone of all healthy relationships, and what is so baffling about the human condition is how fragile and elusive it can be and how quickly we move into and then stay in disconnection. The major problem with disconnectedness is how rarely we recognize it when we're in it, which then leads to staying in it. No wonder marriage and family therapists are busy nowadays. Disconnectedness is rampant in our culture and only getting worse. You may or may not have considered your relationship with God through the lens of your degree of connectedness or disconnectedness, but doing so will profoundly help you as you navigate the gaps.

Let's start with the two shifts.

RELATIONAL DYNAMICS WITH YOURSELF

The first shift is simple enough: we need to add ourselves to our conscious list of relationships. It may sound odd at first, but one key reason we struggle to connect to God is that we are often profoundly disconnected from ourselves. We simply do not see ourselves as one of our core relationships. If someone asked you who is in your family, you would list your immediate family, of course, but I'm guessing you would be down to your great-uncles and second cousins once removed before you ever think to include yourself.

I get it. It feels weird to immediately point to "yourself" when you think of your key relationships, but adding yourself to your conscious list of relationships can actually be transformative to your faith experience. You have been in relationship with yourself for quite a while now, and what happens in that relationship impacts every other relationship you have.

This simple practice has wide-ranging implications. Take, for example, the fact that most of us are kinder to our friends than we are to ourselves. When you reflect on this, you will be startled to see a stark contrast between how you treat your loved ones and how you treat yourself, how you speak to your loved ones and how you speak to yourself.

Let me give you a couple of examples from my own life. I check in on my friends. I ask how they're doing. I believe them when they answer me. In contrast, I tend to neglect myself. I minimize or ignore how I am doing, and I do not give myself permission to be human-sized. I speak to myself in a way I would never speak to a friend. Up until a few years ago, I frequently called myself a "moron" or "stupid" without any regard for myself. I tell myself to get over it and suck it up, but I would never do that to someone I love. You can see this same stark contrast between how you treat yourself and how God treats you, what you say to yourself compared to God's words to you.

Have you ever been in a relationship with someone whose inner critic speaks so loudly that they cannot hear your compliments? You try to tell them that they're an amazing person, but you can tell they have Teflon around their heart, and your compliment ricochets off their protective wall. You have to take cover as your compliment comes flying back at you. Do you know someone who needs constant reassurance about your relationship, and no matter how much encouragement you offer, it is never enough? What about a person who is always hunting for recognition? Maybe you're someone who punishes yourself for making mistakes. You are very patient with others but highly impatient with yourself. Or you are someone who overcommits to people because you struggle with boundaries. You are there for others, but you struggle to ask for help for yourself. Maybe you are someone who overextends again and again and keeps running into a wall of exhaustion.

These are all signs that you have not put yourself on your conscious list of relationships. You would never expect of others what you expect of yourself, nor would you speak to others the way you speak to yourself. Later in this book, we'll see how important this dichotomy is as we carefully examine the contrast between the way we treat and see ourselves and the way God treats and sees us.

Each of us has an inner life that drives us and sometimes disconnects us. That's the human reality, but what we can do is increase our awareness and intentionality to reconnect. We don't do this out of self-centeredness, but as a way to connect to God more deeply.

If you think about the person who cannot receive a compliment or whose inner critic is harsh and unrelenting, the solution isn't for you to speak more loudly or convincingly; it is for them to do the difficult and brave work of bringing those inner messages to the surface and escaping their tenacious grip. After they do that, the odds of your messages of love seeping in increase.

How are we ever going to relax into the love and presence of God if we allow our inner voice to run the show? In the upcoming chapters, we will explore ways to do this, but for now, please pay attention to yourself and give yourself permission to be human-sized. You may well be shocked at how that simple and brave move can open your soul to receiving what God has for you.

Some of us are remarkably unaware of ourselves. I am not naturally aware of myself. I do not consciously think about how I am doing or what I am feeling. I am, however, deeply attuned to others. As a pastor, I delight in taking care of others, but I am less prone to take care of myself or let someone else take care of me. I am particularly resistant to letting God take care of me. I don't like to be a bother. I am uncomfortable with my needs.

When someone used to ask me how I was doing, I would say, "I'm fine, thanks," and just keep pressing on. The truth is, I didn't know the answer. It never occurred to me to think about it. I was too busy pressing forward or focusing on someone else. I should clarify that this did not make me a selfless person. Sometimes focusing on someone else looked like blaming them or being irritated at them. Sometimes it meant I was ignoring my own pain or bypassing my need for rest or care. Focusing on others was an effective tool of avoidance. I finally learned to take responsibility for myself and think about what was going on inside me. Taking responsibility has opened a conduit to a lot of freedom.

About a decade ago, I made a commitment to be more mindful of how I was doing. When someone asked how I was doing, I changed my answer from "I'm fine" to "I don't know" and pressed on to walk my daily treadmill of activity. Not much changed. In the last few years, though, I have tried to pause long enough to discover the true answer to that question. I am often alarmed at what I discover. There is a whole world going on under the surface of my awareness. Sometimes I am infected by all that is going on; sometimes I am infecting others, which may be why someone is asking that question in the first place.

The more I allow myself to be exactly human-sized, the more I bump into God, making space for God instead of filling the space with my incessant need to do or to people-please or to rush in. The more I take seriously that I am in a precious relationship with myself, the healthier I become emotionally and spiritually and the more my soul opens up to God's presence.

So here is tool number one in this book: take seriously your relationship with yourself, and care for yourself the way you care for the people you love. Treat yourself with the same kindness and courtesy you give to others. Check in with yourself the way you check in with your friends and family. Ask yourself, *How are you?* and wait until you know the answer. Remember Jesus' command: "Love your neighbor *as yourself*" (Mark 12:31, emphasis added)—simple words to say, yet difficult to put into action. When we put ourselves on our conscious list of relationships, two foundational shifts happen: (1) we learn to be as kind to ourselves as God is to us, and thus our inner chatter begins to line up with God's truth; and (2) we discover that we can connect with God because we have paused long enough to "be still, and know" that God is God (Psalm 46:10). We become aware of the ways in which all that is within us is blocking our capacity to notice God.

RELATIONAL DYNAMICS WITH GOD

The second shift has to do with the way we see our relationship with God. I am asking you to see your relationship with God the way you see your relationships with other humans. One reason we grapple with gaps between our beliefs and our experience of God is that we tend to put our relationship with God in a whole different category than our relationship with humans. Our human relationships are so much more tangible, aren't they? I struggle to relate to an ever- present but invisible God compared to, say, reaching out for my wife's hand or laughing at a friend's joke.

There are core differences, of course, but the dynamics that infect our human relationships also infect our relationship with God. We are too quick to see our relationship with God as categorically different. It isn't. Some people bypass any sort of faith pursuit and reside in a noncommittal agnosticism because they simply cannot wrap their minds around how to relate to an invisible, intangible God. But what might it look like to relate to God in the same way you relate to people? What if the same issues that cause disconnection between us and our people also come between us and God? Even though God is categorically different from us, the nature of the relationship is actually quite similar.

So far we have two tools in our tool belt that are focused on the way we see our relationships: (1) our obvious but elusive relationship with ourselves and (2) our relationship with God. I'm urging you to see both of these through the same lens you use for all of your other precious relationships. Simple enough.

THE FOUR CORE RELATIONAL DYNAMICS

This is where things get a little more technical. If we can become familiar with the recurring issues that block health in every relationship, we'll be able to notice those same issues in our relationship with ourselves and with God. Every relationship is infected by four core dynamics. However, we struggle to notice them because these dynamics are all we've ever known. Just as fish struggle to think about the water in which they swim, we struggle to notice the relational dynamics in which we exist. Pause to consider how much these four dynamics infect your relational health. Once you notice them and bring them to the surface, you can never unsee them. Then you can learn to lessen their effect, which can increase connection, awareness, and presence with yourself, with God, and with others.

1. ASSUMPTIONS

Assumptions are the way we make meaning out of something we think we know but do not actually know. In every relational struggle in our lives, we've very likely made a string of assumptions about the other person and they have made a few about us. And we also make assumptions about other people's assumptions about us! Some of us are Olympic-level long jumpers in our ability to leap to false conclusions. Assumptions almost always put us in a false reality, an illusion. It is profoundly difficult to relate to humans and to God when we are living in an illusion because we are no longer connecting with them based on what is true. Instead we are living in reactivity and operating out of what we think we know but actually do not know.

Assumptions are fascinating because we think they are absolute until we pause to look at them soberly. And when we do, we discover they are groundless. But even once we know they are groundless, they can linger. I have been chagrined to discover that exposed assumptions can still hold a grip on me. I uncover an assumption or, more commonly, someone helps me see it, and I know it to be an assumption, yet it keeps controlling my thinking.

Assumptions are also contagious. We infect others with our assumptions, and others infect us. When I served as a pastor in Las Vegas, I spent most of my time in crisis intervention, helping people trapped in chronic poverty or who had gotten into trouble quickly. Las Vegas can be a predatory city. Some of these people were understandably desperate and would push my assumption buttons with assumptions of their own. I needed to be needed and wanted to relieve their pressure. I had to rush in and calm them down so I could be calm. I was a pastor working at a large, wealthy church, so they wanted me to take away all their problems by giving them money. In these interactions, we each caught and spread assumptions, and things quickly escalated. This dynamic of contagious assumptions leads to our second dynamic.

2. REACTIVITY

When we do not get what we think we need in a given situation, we get reactive. For me, this happens in dozens of ways—when I feel disrespected, when I witness discourtesy, and when John comes eight minutes late to our team meeting *again* but acts like he's right on time. I get reactive when I feel misunderstood or when I have disappointed someone. I have many triggers, and so do you. It takes very little to get us on the reactivity spiral. Reactivity can feel like we've been thrown onto a treadmill. All of a sudden, we're expending all this energy, but we're not really getting anywhere—a lot of running and not much progress. Reactivity causes us to disconnect—from ourselves, from the people we encounter, and, yes, from an awareness of God's presence.

What are some of your reactivity triggers? You might already know, but if you're not sure, you can begin by noticing three signals: your anger, your shame, and your core values. What makes you angry? What quickly fills you with shame? What happens when someone violates one of your core values? What do you do next? Welcome to your reactivity. If you're still not sure, ask someone who cares about you what they have noticed.

Of course, when they tell you, it helps not to respond reactively! Reactivity is a form of anxiety, and much like assumptions, it is highly contagious. We catch reactivity from one another, which is why some disagreements escalate so quickly. Reactivity from others generates reactivity inside us. I picture each of us carrying an invisible bucket. It doesn't take much for our bucket to overflow with reactivity until we struggle to carry it, so we end up dumping it—usually into someone else's bucket. You can watch reactivity spread in a group, with overflowing buckets dumping into those around you.

Here is one more guide to rooting out reactivity: when we are filled with reactivity, we get either bigger or smaller than human-sized. Sometimes our mama bear comes out, and we stand firm. We dominate, raise our voice, interrupt someone. Sometimes the way we get bigger feels good. As a pastor, I've seen this again and again when people try to care for a grieving person. The grief is so big that it makes the caregiver anxious. We want to help, so we recommend a book or give advice about how to get relief. This is understandable, but it is a sign that we've tried to either grow bigger than the problem or shrink the complexity of the situation to something more manageable with a simple piece of advice. Dads are infamous for doing this with their teen daughters. "There are plenty more fish in the sea, honey." Technically true, but this scores a zero on the helpfulness scale.

Sometimes reactivity makes us smaller than human-sized. We become a turtle that retracts into its shell. We believe we cannot show up fully as ourselves. Maybe you have been in a meeting where you chose not to say what you really thought. You knew your opinion would be dismissed, so you got smaller and didn't show up as your full self. In families, we sometimes see people get smaller because they simply check out and disengage. There is too much heat flying around. Others appease and say, "Fine, have it your way," when they really mean, "I don't have the energy, so I'm quitting." Sometimes getting smaller looks like relieving the tension with a joke. We refuse to sit in the tension, so we say something funny at an inappropriate time. And sometimes we get smaller by charming our way out of a situation. We generally get smaller any time we no longer feel safe to be exactly ourselves and have a subconscious need to protect ourselves.

Some relationships struggle because one person gets bigger when they are reactive and the other person gets smaller. The "bigger" person wants a loud fight, but the "smaller" person needs space. Reactivity breeds reactivity, but it doesn't always look the same.

Reactivity numbs us to God's presence because it is a form of self-dependence. When we get bigger than human-sized, we fill the space where God resides. When we get smaller, we diminish our stature and move into self-protection. Whether we tend toward self-aggrandizement or self-protection, it is difficult to notice God when we are filled with "self." When we are filled with reactivity, we feel like everything is on our shoulders, and we struggle to notice that God is near. We certainly forget that God is active and at work.

Think about the last time you were angry, filled with shame, burdened by all you had to do, afraid to speak your mind. Do you remember a time when someone violated one of your core values? Were you keenly aware of God in those moments? Perhaps the authors of Scripture often command us to "remember the Lord" to counter our situation of being filled with various levels of reactivity. Our invisible buckets are close to overflowing much of the time, so we forget the Lord and keep pressing on through our own efforts.

Reactivity is a cousin of fear, yet it doesn't always feel like fear. When I work with people who tend to get bigger when they are reactive, they struggle to practice being human-sized because years of getting bigger feels so good. It doesn't feel like fear at all; rather, it feels like power and strength. But at a deeper level, it is protecting them from something. It is based on a deeper fear. John reminds us that "perfect love drives out fear" (1 John 4:18). I would add a corollary—fear drives out our awareness of perfect love.

Most humans carry a significant level of reactivity most of the time. Therefore, I encourage you to put yourself on your conscious list of relationships, because when you are reactive without realizing it, you struggle to notice God. It takes intentionality and practice to notice it, name what is driving it, and defuse it so your soul can relax into an awareness of God.

3. STUCK PATTERNS

Stuck patterns happen inside ourselves and in our relationships with others. Do you ever get tired of struggling with a tendency you can't seem to break? I've already mentioned my propensity to rush in and fix or give advice. When someone is venting or sharing about their day, my brain is infected by my assumption that the other person wants my advice, and I never consider sifting that assumption through the filter of what is true. I am sort of drunk in the moment, no longer able to see what the situation requires. I certainly don't pause and ask God for God's insight on the matter. My assumption generates reactivity, and off I go. It is only when someone gets irritated at me or gently says that they were just telling me about their day, not asking for advice, that I "sober up." More often than not, the person just wants someone to listen, but my autopilot lands me in a false reality.

I can't overemphasize how stuck I am in this thinking pattern. I have been aware of it for decades and have even worked in vocations where I was trained to restrain myself from rushing in with advice, and yet it is still my default. It is a stuck pattern of behavior based on deep-seated assumptions.

Stuck patterns block our capacity to encounter God because we operate on autopilot rather than by the power and guidance of God's Holy Spirit. The reality is, while I would like to be someone who is led by the Spirit, most of the time I am unaware of God's Spirit and am led by my own reactivity.

Because these stuck patterns are predictable and recurring, you would think they would be easy to identify and overcome. But while an outside observer can easily spot these stuck patterns, when it's *your* relationship, they're harder to identify because they infect your entire reality with assumptions and reactivity. When couples fight, they often fight in the exact same way, even if the topic of their fight changes. *What* they fight about changes, but *the way* they fight is predictably the same. Each time a fight is resolved, the couple thinks they've solved the problem, but the stuck pattern remains.

Here's another example. Parents are intent on getting their kids out the door for school. The kids oversleep again, thus putting them behind. They did not pack lunches the night before, as Mom has urged, and so they had to scramble, asking for help with lunch, leaving a mess while Mom or Dad have to escalate the situation with a raised voice, speedily ushering them out the door so they are not late. The kids leave with the parent's frustration ringing in their ears, and the parent is frustrated that they had to push again. Both the parents and the kids have so many opportunities to break this cycle, but instead the pattern happens again and again. It is a predictable, recurring pattern.

Part of my job as a leadership consultant is to help leaders notice stuck patterns in their leadership and between their people. It is always easier to see it in others than in yourself. It's a bit wild how long we can perpetuate predictable, repeatable patterns of behavior and never step outside the cycle to notice it.

Our tendency is to focus on other people. *They* are the problem. Why don't *they* change? But if you take seriously the first tool—your relationship with yourself—you may be startled to discover just how much you are contributing to the problem. By changing your side of the stuck pattern, you can create possibilities for change in the relationship. For parents who seek a different experience with their kids in the morning, perhaps they might let their children oversleep and face the school administrators for themselves. Or maybe you expect your five-year-old child to have an adult brain; the reality is that they do not have the human development to manage themselves. By entering into a stuck pattern with curiosity and kindness, you can gently locate the assumptions and reactivity that keep the stuck pattern going. Maybe you discover that your reactivity with your child is connected to your belief about what kind of parent you should be. You are reactive because your child's tardiness reflects poorly on you. Could there be a direct link between your child's behavior and your precious reputation at the school?

Regardless of how many times we encounter stuck patterns, we are often surprised when they happen. When someone with a reputation for tardiness is late to a meeting, no one is surprised—except for the person who shows up late. What is it about chronically late people who are surprised when they're late? They have an assumption about themselves—namely, their ability to check off one more item on their never-ending to-do list. *The meeting starts in twenty minutes*, they say to themselves. *I bet I have time to reroof the house.*

Our relationship with God has many stuck patterns. We hold assumptions about God and what to expect from God, and over time, these assumptions form stuck patterns. This dynamic can be complex because we do not hold them alone; we hold them in community. Those of us in faith communities can infect one another with our own faith assumptions and stuck patterns. Every group resists change over time, so we stifle our capacity to break free from stuck approaches to faith.

I see this a lot when it comes to our personal faith and the Bible. Many of us live out of an assumption that we should point people to a Bible passage they can apply to their lives. Or if someone is sharing something profoundly painful, we are tempted to redirect them to the "bright side." Underneath this practice may be an assumption that we need to defend God, and underneath that assumption, I suspect, is a lot of fear. We are more prone to point to a Bible passage than to help sufferers feel seen and heard.

Another simple example of stuck patterns in our faith communities is in the clichés we pass to each other. You may have heard someone say, "God won't give you more than you can handle." Why are they saying that? It isn't in the Bible. In fact, it is the opposite of what the Bible teaches. Yet some believers say it because of their assumptions and unmanaged reactivity. *I must say something comforting. I must say something to make sense of this terrible thing.*

My church celebrates the Lord's Supper every week, during which we have a time of quiet contemplation. Some people find themselves in a stuck pattern in this simple act—taking the bread and the cup and remembering Jesus' death, burial, and resurrection. As they bow their heads, they don't focus on what God has done for them; they feel guilty that they didn't pray much that week and then pledge to God that they will try harder next week. Next week comes, and the cycle continues. Predictable, recurring, stuck patterns.

You can read through the book of Judges in the Old Testament to see how the people of God were stuck in a predictable, recurring pattern for years. Yet stuck patterns in our relationship with God don't have to be permanent. I believe we can experience relief in our faith if we learn to notice the stuck patterns that affect our relationship with God. Stuck patterns are powerful; they keep us disconnected, expending energy that is unproductive. If we can learn to notice and break them, it can help us connect with God.

4. ATTEMPTED SOLUTIONS

Family therapist Jay Haley famously told his clients, "I don't address problems; I address attempted solutions." We all have problems, and many times we are able to resolve our problems. But some problems are actually made worse by our attempted solutions. For example, someone posts an inflammatory statement on social media, and you become reactive. But you do not know you are reactive. Your reactivity is generated by assumptions you hold about yourself and the person who posted—*that person clearly needs to be corrected, and I'm the one to do it.* You do not realize you are operating out of assumption and reactivity. You are just living your one wild and precious life.

But your brain is deceived in that moment. You are no longer able to see reality, and you become infected by reactivity. So you comment on their post with a corrective response. It may be very direct, or it may be couched in soft language. You believe your comment will help the poster see the error of their ways, or maybe you just enjoy putting people in their place. Whatever your motive, your comment is an attempted solution.

After you reply with your corrective comment, the thread quickly devolves into something like a playground argument. Assumptions and reactivity fly around wildly, and everyone on the thread catches them like viruses. This whole situation is a stuck pattern. And the thing is, this scenario will probably play out again. No wonder social media platforms grow so rapidly—they count on these stuck patterns and attempted solutions to survive.

Maybe as you read this, you're thinking, *That isn't me. I don't stoop down to their level.* In your case, your attempted solution is to feel morally superior to the rest of us. Rather than engage directly, you silently judge everyone on the thread and enjoy being a better person. *Thank you, God, that I am not like those foolish commentators.*

DISPELLING THE ILLUSION

Every relationship has stuck patterns and attempted solutions. If you are married, maybe you've raised an issue with your spouse, and they offered a testy reply. Your attempted solution was to prove your point. Before you knew it, the discussion escalated into uncontrolled reactivity. One of you got hysterical and made a lot of generalizations; the other got historical and brought up past wounds. You lost connection with each other and with reality. You were more intent on winning than loving, being heard than listening, protecting yourself from harm than healing the relationship.

What happened? Assumptions, reactivity, and stuck patterns infected your relationships. Your attempted solutions kept you from moving forward or made everything worse. As a general rule, an *attempted* solution to a problem forms a stuck pattern. For those still intent on getting their kids out the door on time, you could go back to the early encounters and map out the solutions you tried, which may have helped keep the stuck patterns going.

Some of you are stuck in patterns with family members. Maybe you have a relative or immediate family member who is simply unreasonable, and the rest of the family go along with their bad behavior because "it is just their way." Your attempted solution is to let them get away with their unreasonable demands and behavior. As long as they get away with it, and as long as you pay the emotional price for it, you will be in a stuck pattern. Your attempted solutions of worrying about it, expending energy wondering how to manage them, and calling other family members to explain their behavior and keep a false peace are the dynamics that keep the stuck pattern alive.

You can see why family therapists stay busy. These core dynamics infect and damage every precious relationship we have, and they are the primary dynamics that marriage and family therapists look for to help people get along better.

I believe we struggle with gaps in our relationship with God because of these four dynamics. We do not cultivate a relationship with ourselves, so we do not know what is going on in us. We do not consider that our relationship with God has dynamics that are similar to those of our human relationships. We bring assumptions, reactivity, stuck patterns, and attempted solutions into our relationship with God that keep us from encountering God because they put us in a false reality. This is why we grapple with a chasm between what we believe and what we experience.

I freely admit we are not solely to blame for the gaps. God brings some unique challenges to the relationship. God is invisible, which makes God hard to relate to in a tangible way. When we read our Bible, especially the Gospels, we see God using vocal cords, but when we try to listen to God today, we often hear silence or a gentle prompting. Often we have to *infer* what God is doing and saying. Jesus' resurrection, the linchpin of our faith, happened a long time ago, and if we're honest, some of us wonder if Jesus really is coming back one day. We believe God is all-powerful and also all-loving and all-knowing, but God does not intervene as often as we would like or in the ways we would like. God can do so but doesn't. It stings. It is hard to reconcile. So, yes, some of the challenges in our relationship with God come from God's side.

But God holds no false assumptions about us. God is not easily triggered. God is free from getting stuck. God exists in reality. So the problematic relational dynamics come only from us—from our assumptions about ourselves and about God, our triggers that block awareness of God, our stuck patterns, and our attempted solutions—all infecting us and keeping us in a false reality. In reality, this is good news because we can take responsibility for our side of the relationship and work on managing the infectious dynamics and perhaps then experience the encounters we long for.

As I mentioned in the introduction, I had an epiphany in 2016 that will forever shift the way I see my faith. If the heart of assumptions, stuck patterns, and reactivity is *something false*, it puts us in an illusion. But God is truth. God exists in concrete reality, and when we live in reality and truth, we can more easily access God's presence. But these relational dynamics keep us in a false reality and lead us to miss God all too often.

Jesus says we have the capacity to know truth, and when we know what is true and live into what is true, we are set free. We can connect with and be fully present to ourselves, others, and God. Thankfully, I've found some tools that can help us move from unhealthy relational dynamics into healthy dynamics. We'll look a little closer at these tools and the toolbox they come from—systems theory—in the next chapter. By using them to learn more about the truth of who we are and how we relate to God, we can dispel the illusion and relax into the presence of God, our souls fully open to God's manifest presence.

DISCUSSION QUESTIONS

If you are in a discussion group, provide ground rules that will create a safe space for everyone to share openly. If you are prone to advising and fixing, if you struggle to hear someone's pain without feeling pain yourself, or if you get anxious in silence, this would be a good time to declare it so your group can gently help you manage it.

1. What do you think of the idea of putting yourself on your list of relationships?
2. How might being kind to yourself help you encounter God's kindness?
3. What assumptions do you hold about God or about yourself that might be blocking your connection with God?
4. What situations make you reactive? Do you typically get bigger or smaller than human-sized?
5. When you are reactive, do you struggle to notice God's presence?
6. Can you name any stuck patterns you see in your faith or in your human relationships?
7. Attempted solutions can be hard to identify. Do any attempted solutions come to mind?

TWO

RELAXING INTO GOD'S PRESENCE

We all are born into the world looking for someone looking for us, and we remain in this mode of searching for the rest of our lives.
CURT THOMPSON, *THE SOUL OF SHAME*

If you want to connect deeply with God, you first have to connect deeply with yourself. Do you find that idea jolting? I did the first time I encountered it. It challenges the way I'm wired. It felt selfish and foreign to make this shift. I had always oriented around the idea of emptying or denying myself, but I learned slowly that the best path to focusing on others and connecting with God was to first focus on myself.

When I began this practice, I was overwhelmed by all I discovered in me. No wonder I focused so much on others. Focusing on myself was painful. But how can I empty myself, deny myself, and die to self if I am completely unaware of myself? Paul tells us in Romans 12:1–2 that we can give ourselves to God as living sacrifices, and in exchange, God will renew our minds. The more aware I am of what is in me, the more power I have to give it to God as a living sacrifice, and the more God renews my mind. "Love God and love your neighbor" has a pesky appendix—"as you love yourself." Can you actually love God and your neighbor if you do not love yourself or if you are not aware of the dynamics going on in yourself?

In the previous chapter, I invited you to put yourself on your conscious list of relationships. The simplest tool to help with this is to write down three or four specific habits you do for your friends and loved ones and three or four things you say to them to express your care and love. For me, I call my friends to check on how they are doing. When they share, I listen to them. I am kind to them and take seriously what is going on in their lives. I enjoy them. I use encouraging words to show them I believe in them. These things are obvious and occur regularly among loved ones. But if I consider the way I treat myself and talk to myself, I see a stark contrast. I call myself stupid or a moron. I am quite harsh with myself. I neglect my own needs rather than checking in on how I am doing. I often struggle to allow my friends to care for me. You can do this exercise too. You might use a table like this:

WHAT I DO FOR MY LOVED ONES	WHAT I SAY TO MY LOVED ONES	WHAT I DO FOR OR SAY TO MYSELF

It is quite a stark contrast, isn't it? Why are we so kind to others and so harsh to ourselves? This week, practice some simple self-kindness, taking time to check in on yourself, being as gentle with yourself as you are with others you love.

My thesis is this: the best and only gift you have to offer to God and your people is a well self. Of course, a "well self" sounds like a destination. You might rightly be cautious and say, "Whoa, Nelly! If I wait until I am well, I will never actually offer anything!" In this approach though, "well" is not a destination; it is an intentional journey. I am on the journey of being well by putting myself on my conscious list of relationships and by noticing the dynamics that affect my connection with God. Wellness, then, is a path on which we can take baby steps.

You may still have trouble processing that I'm proposing you offer a "well self" rather than offering Jesus. Your reaction may be, *Who cares about offering myself? Surely Jesus is the best and only thing I have to offer.* To this I say that the best chance you have to offer Jesus to people is for you to first walk down the path toward being well.

We have all seen the colossal damage caused by unwell religious people who attempt to offer Jesus to others. Those situations become big news when they involve famous Christian leaders. When their private behaviors are exposed, many of these leaders move into denial or minimize what they have done, which makes their behavior more damaging to people. Through this process, religious leaders who are unwell do more damage to others and also to their own souls, all because they refused to address their own triggers and issues. At some point in their faith journey, they did not believe they could be human-sized. They let their reactivity and triggers get the better of them. Their attempted solution was to hide and blame. What might their lives have looked like if they had cultivated a relationship with themselves, paying attention to the dynamics under the surface and doing the deeper, more difficult work?

Most of us are not famous enough to make the news with our sickness, but the same dynamic can happen to us. We infect people and are infected by them when we do not first do the difficult work of paying attention to ourselves. We offer Jesus before we spend time actually connecting with Jesus. By working toward emotional wellness and fighting for freedom, we can transmit a healthy representation of Jesus.

I am fascinated by the question Jesus asked the paralyzed man who had been unwell for thirty-eight years: "Do you want to get well?" (John 5:6). Surely that man must have been thinking, *Well, over the course of thirty-eight years, it crossed my mind a time or two.* But that question from Jesus pierces my own soul. I have carried some unnecessary conditions for longer than thirty-eight years that Jesus is offering to heal.

So Jesus asks me, "Do you want to get well?"

I want to be well, and that means I want to live in reality. I want to be set free by the truth that Jesus promises. I want people to hunger for Christ when they see my life. I would like to pour out my life as an offering to Christ. I would like to be a jar of clay that God's Spirit flows through freely. That means I have work to do, especially around my assumptions, reactivity, stuck patterns, and attempted solutions. I must do the uncomfortable work of paying attention to all the ways my own self gets in the way of connecting with God's presence. This is an ongoing and lifelong work. The journey of wellness takes a lot of patience and self-kindness.

I derived these four relational dynamics from something called *systems theory*, the science of healthy and unhealthy relational patterns. Marriage and family therapists use systems theory in their work, but I believe we can apply these same dynamics to our relationship with God.

I was introduced to systems theory when I served as a trauma and hospice chaplain after college. You can imagine how helpful these tools were for an anxious young chaplain eager to prove himself. I was overwhelmed by the onslaught of grief and death all around me. It generated deep emotion inside me that I didn't know I was carrying. Before chaplaincy I would have described myself as a typical

Australian—laid-back, relaxed, unfazed. But the constant barrage of death, trauma, and serious medical conditions peeled back that veneer to expose a bubbling volcano of triggers and fears.

I found systems theory helpful in managing myself, reducing my own reactivity, and helping families manage the worst moments of their lives because it gave me a way to notice anxiety spreading—first in me and then in the families I worked with. My time as a chaplain was a boot camp for discovering assumptions, reactivity, stuck patterns, and attempted solutions. Boot camp is over, but I am still enlisted in this way of being.

After my stint as a chaplain, I was hooked on systems theory. It unlocked so much inside me and helped me make sense of dynamics in my life I was previously blind to. I studied this theory more in graduate school, where my counseling professor exposed me to a wider set of systems tools. I have been studying, refining, and teaching it for decades now. While you do not need a comprehensive understanding of systems theory to address the faith gaps covered in this book, a little bit of background will help show its power to dispel illusions in our relationships and its potential for strengthening our relationship with God.

SYSTEMS THEORY

In the 1960s, a psychiatrist named Murray Bowen developed a new systems theory that focused on the family as the patient—as a single emotional unit—rather than focusing on one individual. In that era, parents brought their depressed teen for treatment, and the therapist focused only on the teen. In his approach, Bowen not only treated the teen, whom he called the "identified patient," but he invited the whole family to be part of the therapeutic process. He carefully watched how the family interacted to try to discern why the teen was exhibiting depression symptoms. Perhaps the teen's depression was a symptom of the parents' marriage, for example, or because of the teen's challenges in coping with a highly successful sibling. (We do not often think about the siblings of famous athletes, but for every world-champion athlete in this world, you can be assured that there are a lot of neglected siblings!)

Bowen began his noticing journey when he worked in a psychiatric lockdown unit in the 1950s. He would observe stuck patterns on parent visitation day. His typical patient was a young man with teenage-onset schizophrenia. These young men were quite large, and you can imagine the difficulty their mothers had wrangling them through their teen years before handing them over to the state. On visitation day, Bowen watched these petite mothers walk toward their sons with arms out for a hug with body language that was tentative, which communicated fear. The son could read the tentative, fearful posture and proceeded to give their mother a tentative hug in return. Bowen watched the mothers look at their sons and say, "What's the matter? Aren't you glad to see me?" He realized these mixed messages can generate pathology in us if we don't know how to interpret them. (Incidentally, narcissistic and abusive people often use mixed messages to keep their victims off-balance.)

Bowen postulated eight concepts to explain human behavior and relationships, mostly around the themes of contagious anxiety and family dynamics. He did groundbreaking work on generational traits—the way we each hold generational behaviors and those behaviors grab hold of us. Bowen generated a "genogram"—a "family tree" of sorts that focuses on generational patterns, emotional bonds, and binds.

When I was a chaplain, my colleagues and I spent a lot of time discussing the Bowen theory—systems theory—because the head chaplain was one of Bowen's early students. As soon as he began to teach us how to view anxiety, I was forever changed. I quickly saw it in myself and also how it infected the families I served. I did my own genogram and was struck by how many patterns and assumptions had me in their grip from my own family of origin.

Another of Bowen's ideas that has shaped my own understanding of relationships is his cornerstone concept—*differentiation of self.* Differentiation is the tricky skill of functioning as an emotionally healthy individual while staying emotionally connected to other people—in other words, staying in healthy relationships without spreading or catching anxiety and also without distancing or detaching from those people. It involves getting clear on your own vision and values, defining ("differentiating") yourself when someone else wants to wrap you up into their own sense of self. You may be familiar with the concept of codependency or enmeshment—the simple idea, "When Momma ain't happy, ain't nobody happy." Differentiation is the difficult skill of connecting with unhappy Momma without being unhappy yourself.

Bowen taught that we can stop focusing on the other person and all that they are doing, and instead take responsibility for ourselves. When we do so, we can change our relational patterns with the other person. Bowen saw pathology not as existing independently in any one person; rather, he believed that a person's behavior is a symptom of a sick *system* of people.

In Bowen's early experiments, he did family therapy not just with his individual patients but with their siblings, parents, and grandparents as well—even uncles, aunts, and cousins. Bowen may have gone overboard in his crowded therapy sessions, but his experiments helped us understand family dynamics—the ways we affect and infect each other even down through the generations of our families. You can see this as you read the Bible, especially in the Hebrew Scriptures. Abraham's trait of deception was passed down to Isaac, who deceived a king much the same way his dad had done (see Genesis 12:10–20; 20:1–18; 26:7–9). That deception comes to the forefront in his grandson Jacob, who cheats his brother out of his family blessing (see Genesis 25:29–34). And don't get me started on how King David's behavior was transmitted to his children, who lived dysfunctional and anxious lives.

Bowen's other breakthrough was to help us understand a particular type of anxiety called "chronic anxiety." These days, we talk more about anxiety than we used to, but the prevalence of anxiety is increasing. One reason is that we do not talk about specific types of anxiety. Anxiety comes in many forms, and each has its own playbook. Acute anxiety, trauma, and grief are all generated by something real, but chronic anxiety is generated by something false, or a *perceived need*. If we can learn what makes us chronically anxious, if we can learn our triggers and false needs, then we can manage them instead of watching them get the better of us. We can lower reactivity and increase connection and awareness.

Marriage and family therapists have been using Murray Bowen's theory (or a version of it) for decades, and it is commonly taught in counseling programs and in some seminaries. Systems theory helped me as a chaplain and as a pastor. I saw how I affected systems by bringing my own anxiety, reactivity, and assumptions into every encounter. It also helped me quickly assess the dynamics between family members, which was invariably heightened by sickness and trauma.

In the decades since Bowen's groundbreaking work, many have taken Bowen's initial theory in all kinds of fascinating directions, including studying how we form and break stuck relational patterns. One fascinating recent adaption of Bowen's theory is called internal family systems (IFS)—each person has a Self (inner parent) that consists of an undetermined number of "parts." It builds on the simple and stunning idea that you as an individual are actually a system because you have parts of yourself that can get in the way of each other. The part that wants to fight can conflict with the part that wants to run away. The part that wants to get things done competes with the part that wants to lie down on the couch. It is the wisdom of the IFS approach that inspired me to challenge you to add yourself to your list of relationships. If you can locate what is happening inside you and attend to it or, more powerfully, invite God to attend to it, you can truly experience freedom and relief.

Feel free to explore systems theory on your own. At the end of the book, I provide an appendix of resources for further reading and research. It can be helpful to know the theory behind the concepts, but my ultimate goal is not to teach you systems theory. Rather, my goal is to equip you with some of its tools to help you with your faith. Let's look at a few of them now.

TOOLS TO OPEN YOUR SOUL TO GOD

Just as some relational dynamics keep us trapped and stuck, other powerful dynamics help us relax into the presence of God (and yes, these same dynamics can help us improve our human relationships as well). As we dig into each gap we will cover throughout this book, I encourage you to utilize one or more of these postures and tools. They are fairly intuitive and don't need much explanation; they mostly need intentionality and practice.

PAUSE

I am still surprised by how much discipline it takes to pause rather than stay stuck in my more-of-the-same and try-harder cycles. Something insidious tells me to keep pressing forward because I believe all the energy and effort is getting me somewhere. But it is not. If I pause after I notice an assumption or stuck pattern, I discover I am on a treadmill to nowhere. Once I get off that treadmill, I can remember the Lord.

At several points throughout this book, you will benefit from pausing and connecting with God rather than turning the page.

You might ask how long you should pause. The goal is to pause long enough to increase awareness—awareness of yourself and of God. Do you know what is going on in you? Can you articulate it to God or to someone else? This is simple, difficult, and essential. I have found that a pause somewhere between two minutes and seven months does the trick! Sometimes I need only a few moments to locate myself; sometimes I need deeper, longer work.

Pausing also increases the chance that love can sneak past our protective layer. Curt Thompson tells us that it takes less than three seconds for our brains to encode a memory of shame, while it takes anywhere from thirty to ninety seconds to encode a memory of love and joy.[1] Could it be that we struggle to encounter God because we do not pause long enough for our soul to move past all that's squeezing it so we can relax into the presence of God? Pausing helps us move past that initial blockage of shame to unlock the floodgates of love and presence.

REFLECTION AND DEBRIEFING

The most powerful training we received as chaplains came from reflection and debriefing. The supervisors never actually taught us how to be chaplains. Rather, they sent us into the wards every day to serve people and then hosted us for ninety minutes every morning as we reviewed the day before and reflected on how we showed up, what got in the way, and what was going on in us. This daily rhythm of serving, then debriefing and reflecting, then serving again caused us to grow and change and become effective chaplains.

The education model on which this training is based is known as Action-Reflection-Action. Go do it, then reflect and talk about it, and then go do it again. Most of us are accustomed to the more traditional "learn about it and then go do it" model. Jesus used Action-Reflection-Action most famously when he sent out his disciples two by two (see Mark 6:7). They packed for the journey, and he unpacked them. Then he sent them with just their wits and God's Spirit to go with them. When they returned, they debriefed how it went.

Most of us will not be able to integrate the tools and practices in

---

1. This insight was shared by Dr. Curt Thompson in a message titled "Bringing Beauty to Chaos," If:Gathering 2022 (Alameda, CA, March 4–5, 2022), https://calvaryalameda.org/media/cf89g83/session-4-bringing-beauty-to-chaos.

this book in real time. We will do better to go out and do, then intentionally reflect and debrief, and then go out and be more aware of how we're showing up. We will have the best experience if we can reflect and debrief with a trusted group in a regular rhythm.

RADICAL SELF-ACCEPTANCE

Over the years, I have learned to pay attention to how harsh I am to myself. I am certainly much harsher to myself than I would ever be to another person. What is that about? And in the church, why do we reinforce this sort of behavior in the name of humility? For some reason, we think God wants us always on the back foot, lest we slip into pride. The fact is, I am harsher to myself than God is to me. What if I were as kind to myself as God is to me? Self-kindness is not about self-actualization or need for approval. It is not a quenching of the Holy Spirit. It is keeping my soul open long enough for the love of God to seep in. It begins with self-acceptance and kindness. Love your neighbor *as yourself.*

PERMISSION

The posture of permission is closely related to, yet slightly different from, self-acceptance. My default posture is to refuse to give myself permission to be human or to feel my feelings. As a pastor, I have never gotten used to the vitriolic feedback a handful of people enjoy sending a pastor's way. This experience was difficult at first, but it became more difficult when I kept getting hurt by it. I thought I would and should grow out of that, but to grow out of being hurt is to grow out of being human.

I am also around an unusual amount of death, sickness, and loss. I get tired of death. Sometimes I just want to opt out of the next intense pastoral encounter. Again, a human is allowed to be tired or want to avoid these kinds of situations, but in my pastoral role, I fundamentally do not believe I am allowed to be human. Permission is huge in practicing being exactly human-sized, which is where the noticing of God's presence begins.

CURIOSITY

My friend Trisha Taylor says, "The opposite of anxiety is not calm; it is curiosity." I am fascinated by that. Curiosity helps us locate assumptions and keep judgment in check. It helps us explore what is beyond what we think we know for sure. Curiosity may be *the* superpower for spiritual growth. Without it, we *assume* we know something. With it, we're unlocked from our rigid assumptions and can move into a life of faith in the one true God. Curiosity requires its cousin—faith—to see what is beyond the horizon of our judgments and assumptions. It also works well with radical self-acceptance. Together they can help us unlock much of what has us bound and stuck.

TESTING ASSUMPTIONS

Over and over, Jesus said, "You have heard that it was said . . . But I tell you . . ." (see Matthew 5:21–48). Might this be the path to spiritual transformation? In the first half of our lives, we assume spiritual transformation comes from learning. Later we discover that unlearning is its own essential journey, and it begins with testing what we always thought was so.

The Stories We Tell Ourselves are sometimes vastly different from the way things are.[2]

God has much for us beyond what we think we know for sure. Faith is required, and so is courage, but it all begins with assumptions. We can also offer this gift to a friend. It is difficult to distinguish between assumptions and the truth. Learn to listen for assumptions in another person and invite them to test them with you. Be curious, ask questions, and listen for hard-edged and extreme language. Extreme and absolute words like *must*, *always*, *never*, and other generalizations are often a sign that someone is living out of assumptions.

---

2. These concepts will be unpacked in the next chapter.

LAUGHTER

Laughter and playfulness are drastically underutilized in spiritual growth. Earnestness can get in the way of soul connection, but laughter opens our souls to wonder and gives us a reprieve from burden. We might look at the many broken places in the world and in our lives and wonder what there is that we could ever laugh about, but I work with people who combat some of the most gut-wrenching poverty and evil you can imagine. I can say as a blanket generalization that these amazing people are quick to laugh, find joy, and celebrate the small pleasures amid grinding, difficult work.

Laughter increases my capacity to do difficult work. It gives me a much-needed breather. I look for ways to laugh multiple times per day, and I intentionally find ways to be playful. Playfulness by definition cannot be productive. If we struggle to be playful, we may need to enlist a child to help us. Playfulness comes naturally to kids, and we are God's kids, so it is good to play for play's sake. Only then can we discover the surprising benefit of play and laughter—opening our soul to God.

TIME

God redeemed us, yes, but I wish redemption went more quickly! Some spiritual growth is miraculous and immediate, but most of it is slow and time-consuming. We keep running into ourselves and can get discouraged, but adding a dose of time to the tools above can bring profound change. The tools in this book are designed to unlock some deep changes that take time to forge. It will take a while to see change. Be as patient with yourself as God is.

INTENTIONALITY

I live much of my life somewhere between being wrapped up in myself and being completely oblivious. My life's momentum is constantly directed toward distraction and hurry. I find myself waking up already thinking about pressing matters, always feeling like there is more to do or jumping from email to social media to television. The good news about intentionality is that we only need a mustard seed's worth to experience transformation. I recommend intentionally cultivating the practice of relaxing into God's presence in the morning and evening, as well as cultivating the tools and postures above.

DISCUSSION QUESTIONS

1. What intense situations have revealed to you what is bubbling underneath the surface in your life? What was that revelation like for you?
2. As you consider the way you treat your loved ones versus the way you treat yourself, what differences or similarities do you find?
3. What could change for you if you began to treat yourself kindly?
4. Where have you seen anxiety become contagious within a group?
5. Which of the postures and tools can you try this week?
6. Which of the postures and tools do you think you will struggle with the most?

THREE

GAP 1: GOD'S PARTICULAR LOVE

"I Believe God Loves Me, but I Don't Feel It"

How do I get the stuff that I believe deepest in my head down into my bloodstream? That is the question that we never stop asking.

TYLER STATON, SERMON TITLED "EPHESIANS: IMMEASURABLY MORE," AUGUST 7, 2022

It is difficult, isn't it, to experience God's love? I'm not sure we talk about this enough. I was shocked the first time I really experienced God's love in a visceral way. It was quite scary and painful to stand in God's presence and receive love without condition or pretense, without control or entitlement. After that initial fear, I experienced a wonderful flood of relief. It was actually quite healing. But before it was healing, it was terrifying because I felt so vulnerable and exposed, with too much potential to be rejected.

I had already believed God loved me in a generic way. I knew God loved humanity, and I was a member of humanity, so therefore

God must love me. But it took me longer to experience God's particular love—the discomfort of standing in God's presence followed by a sensation of peace and relaxation I never knew was possible. Why did it take me so long to get to that point? I had a number of beliefs that were fundamentally protecting me from vulnerability, pain, and threat. I had to learn to let down my guard so I could let love in.

The most likely obstacles we face in encountering God's particular love for us are The Stories We Tell Ourselves.

The Stories We Tell Ourselves are filled with firm assumptions we hold about ourselves, God, and The Way Things Are. Some of these assumptions are so rigidly locked in place, we never pause to wonder if they are true. If we can learn to clarify these assumptions and sift them through God's truth, we can experience profound relief in our faith.

In 2016, I was fly-fishing in the Blue River at Silverthorne, Colorado, when I was overcome by a shame storm. I have always been slow to learn new things, and even though I had fly-fished for a few years, I still could not reliably catch trout. Fly-fishing is a life-giving habit for me. It is a tangible expression of God's love—the beautiful Colorado outdoors, a trout's unique spot pattern, the relaxation of being knee-deep in a stream, the rhythm of the cast, all of it. But my whole life, I have dealt with an underlying belief that I am stupid. And so when I cannot catch actively feeding fish, my inner narrative kicks in pretty loudly. On this particular day, everyone around me was catching fish, but no matter what I tried, I could not interest a fish. My inner critic spoke a clear message to me that day: *See how stupid you are? You are so stupid that you can't even outsmart a tiny-brained fish. Everyone else can do it. You can't do it.*

I was forty-five years old, and my inner critic was still treating me like a little boy in trouble. What is it about the inner critic that has such a powerful hold on our lives?

Our inner critic is the voice of condemnation that speaks anytime we let ourselves down, anytime we do not live up to our own standards. When I am fishing, I expect to be skilled enough to catch fish. When I can't catch them, even though they are clearly biting, I feel stupid. When I feel stupid, I feel exposed. When I see everyone around me catching fish like it is the easiest thing in the world, my shame increases. My inner critic freely speaks into the gap between what I can do and what others can do.

Most of us are aware of our inner critic. The issue isn't awareness; it is that we so freely let it have its way with us. We don't pause to examine its message or its profound impact. We just adopt it wholesale and assume we have to live with it. We give it free rein in our soul, and we let it get away with terrible behavior. We let our inner critic speak to us in a tone and with words we would never use with another person. Some people's inner critic is so harsh and pervasive that they struggle to discern the difference between the voice of their inner critic and the voice of God. Some assume God is as condemning as their inner critic.

I have spent the last decade keenly listening to my inner critic, understanding its core messages, working to sift its words through God's words to see who is telling the truth. My inner critic has three core, recurring messages:

1. You should know better by now.
2. You are stupid and exposed. You cannot do it.
3. You are not worth loving.

When you see the messages of my inner critic listed plainly like that, what comes to mind for you? When I share the message of my inner critic with someone, they often feel compelled to correct it. "Oh, no, that's not true at all, Steve. You are not stupid, and you're worth loving." They are compelled to speak against the message deep within me. That is the insidious nature of our inner critic. We recognize and speak against it in others, but we give it free rein in ourselves. We even assume that letting our inner critic speak harshly to us is a godly way to live—that we are being humble. It is *not* a godly way to live.

Have you ever taken your inner critic out to give it a sober examination? Is it telling you the truth? Is it giving you what you need? Most vitally, does your inner critic's view of you contradict God's view of you?

THE STORIES WE TELL OURSELVES AND THE WAY THINGS ARE

Our inner critic is one of several task force members within our soul who serve on The Stories We Tell Ourselves committee. We may or may not be aware of this committee. The members mostly work undercover, but together they create two core messages: (1) The Stories We Tell Ourselves and (2) The Way Things Are. These messages are a complex web of untested assumptions and thinking patterns that form our deepest core beliefs. The committee means well. It exists and speaks to protect us from vulnerability and hurt, and it is forged from experience, especially childhood experience.

Our inner critic, for example, is often trying to beat others to the punch, condemning us internally so we will change or guard ourselves from outside criticism. It is the Department of Defense for your soul, and it often lives at DEFCON 3, which is one reason you are often weary. We have a hypervigilant Defense Department always scanning for threats and harm, ready to protect us. The problem is, The Stories We Tell Ourselves committee cannot discern true threats. Instead, it issues a blanket covering, so it also keeps out God's words. That is where we need relief. I have found that if I can help the committee stand down, it not only allows God's truth to seep into my soul, but it also helps me be resilient and handle actual threats from others.

As long as The Stories We Tell Ourselves and The Way Things Are remain unexamined, unexposed, and unspoken, we will struggle to encounter God's love. That is because this committee forms core beliefs that are more foundational than even our beliefs about God. As we discussed previously, our beliefs about God may be our most precious beliefs, but The Stories We Tell Ourselves and The Way Things Are form our deepest beliefs. We often give more weight to those beliefs than we do to God, especially if those beliefs run on autopilot. One of the challenges of working with these beliefs is that we don't even know they are beliefs. They are just . . . well . . . The Way Things Are.

But what if everything we believe isn't true? What if The Way Things Are puts us in a false reality and blocks our capacity to encounter God's particular love for us? What if The Stories We Tell Ourselves keep us from encountering God in a soul-satisfying way? We can bring those beliefs to the surface and sift them through our beliefs in God. This is where the work of detangling our precious beliefs from our deepest core beliefs can genuinely help us experience a breakthrough.

The dangerous thing about these beliefs is that they are difficult to articulate. We often don't even know we have them. If you had asked me directly, "Do you think you are worthy of God's love?" I would have replied, "Of course! God's love is freely given, unconditionally, not because of my worth but because of God's worth." But under that belief lies a deeper belief that was hard to avoid. Our deepest core beliefs can be difficult to uncover because they are subconscious. They have been with us since our early memories, and they are fierce in protecting us from pain or lack. So as adults, we have been living with them and depending on them for decades without considering their negative impact or whether they are even true. Many of us have commingled these beliefs with our belief in God, and we struggle to discern between self-protective beliefs and actual truth from God.

With a bit of insight and a lot of courage, we can detangle the various strands that make up The Stories We Tell Ourselves, and we can be suspicious of The Way Things Are long enough to let the truth of God's love seep in. This is brave work; we have to get comfortable with being uncomfortable, but if we can do this, our soul can open up to what is really true.

THE COMMITTEE MEMBERS

Our inner critic serves on this committee. Who else is there? Each of us has a few members in common, and we'll get to those below. But each of us also has committee members that are unique to us, based on our particular, unique life experiences.

YOUR UNIQUE COMMITTEE MEMBERS

As I learned to identify my own committee, I was surprised to discover two members not everyone has. I call one of them the "it's all downhill from here" guy. He is always looking over my shoulder, waiting for something bad to happen because my life has been surrounded by death and tragedy, but not much of it has visited my household. This committee member is always warning me not to celebrate good things because if I do, then something bad will happen. It is a highly superstitious task force member, which is weird because I am not superstitious in any way.

Another member serves as my prayer editor. Every time I pray for someone to be healed, he sends up a warning flare to not get my hopes up. This guy submitted his résumé to join the committee when I was a hospital chaplain. In that intense season, I prayed for healing for so many patients who subsequently died that it hurt my heart to continue to pray that way. My prayer editor urges me to never count on God for anything so God can never let me down. I rationalize that God does not owe me anything, and therefore

I should never expect anything. You can imagine how he might infect my faith in God. I have had to work through cynicism and skepticism when I hear stories of God's healing. I have even had some profound personal encounters with God that this committee member has said were not from God.

Some people have committee members who operate like soldiers. They do not have a desk job in our Defense Department. They are out in the field, scanning for threats in every environment, triggering us to be hypervigilant. These soldiers reported for duty after a significant trauma or abuse in our past, and they've rarely taken leave from their posts. The problem with these soldiers is, they struggle to discern true threats from perceived threats; they trigger us in both, blocking out love and connection from healing humans and from God.

Maybe you carry trauma or come from a history of abuse, and you are hyperaware of its impact, but you struggle to manage it. You feel as if the soldiers are managing you. You find yourself frequently triggered and struggle to experience peace—times when you can stand down, relax, and be exactly yourself. I am mindful of the limits of what a book can do, and I am not clinically trained in trauma. I do not believe a person can simply read their way to healing when they have to deal with these soldiers on their committee.

I am also aware of the complexity of trauma and abuse that can be connected to our faith life. If your experience happened inside a faith community or if you felt abandoned by God, the result can be a dramatic empowerment for the soldiers. This is very tender ground, and I can only hope you will entrust yourself to a trained trauma expert who can help your soldiers stand down once in a while so you can experience some relief. Skilled experts are trained to help you remember trauma or abuse without reliving it in your body as much. They can help lower the intensity of the trigger and reduce the number of triggering situations. I make this sound easier and simpler than it is. It is, in fact, a brave and difficult journey, but the fight for freedom and relief is worth it. You are worth it. You are worth fighting for.

I would also gently suggest that for many people who carry trauma, getting professional help is something they may need to do again and again. They may not always need to be in therapy, but it is common and healthy to enter into seasons of therapy. Many people I know who carry significant trauma want to graduate from it as soon as possible. I wish it worked that way. Trauma is more something to keep peeling and working on. Breaks between the work can be vital, but I hope you will go back for more help if you have not sought help in a while and your triggers have become more activated.

Some people have a religious committee member that reinforces a false story about God and Jesus. These members are particularly insidious because they forge a false belief right in the midst of our church experience. I am not necessarily blaming the church for this. It is true that too many faith communities reinforce legalism, or even worse, spiritual abuse. But we can forge false beliefs even in healthy faith communities. We can take a seemingly innocuous compliment like, "Your family was there every time the doors were open," and turn it into a stronghold like, "I must always be available. I must overextend myself for my church."

My faith community was profoundly welcoming and loving to me when I became a Christian in my teen years, but my family of origin propaganda intertwined with my church experience and caused me to develop unhealthy patterns of hyper-responsibility. I believed I had to be at every event and be there for everyone whenever they had a need. This may have had more to do with my teenage brain than the church, but I have had to examine these core messages—which is the whole point of this chapter. We are not looking for who to blame and are not only focusing on negative experiences; we are examining our beliefs and the meaning we have made from our experiences to see which of those are at odds with the gospel, therefore blocking our capacity to experience God.

Too many people let their religious committee member send them into rapid deconstruction. How many people had an unhealthy relationship with a purity ring? How many sat under the teaching of a spiritually immature but well-meaning youth leader? How many encountered a spiritually abusive or manipulative leader? How many got burned by the unspoken secret agreements of what is acceptable and unacceptable in a church? Far too many followers of Jesus have had to grapple with shame, doubt, fear, and deep mistrust because of their religious experience. They are on a journey that takes courage and patience. It turns out that unlearning can be as fundamental to following Jesus as learning.

OUR COMMON COMMITTEE MEMBERS

We may have different committee members, but we all have three members in common. We've looked at the inner critic. Let's look at two others to see how they forge a bad-news story, flesh out how they generate our deepest core beliefs, and discover how those beliefs block our capacity to experience God's love.

We will start with the family of origin propagandist. This committee member takes assumptions and overt messages you have gained from your family of origin and forms them into core beliefs. I have gained many wonderful assets from my family of origin, and I am proud to have been raised in my family. They gave me the gift of adventure, wonder, and curiosity. They gave me a strong work ethic and a sense of moral duty. Many of my hobbies and pleasures are directly linked to my family of origin—including my love for music and motor racing and my sense of humor.

But even if we were raised in a loving family, we still inherited assumptions and expectations that, if untested and unexamined, can forge a strong set of beliefs that can block our capacity to encounter God's love. Looking into the family of origin propagandist isn't about blame or victimizing ourselves; it is about examining assumptions and uncovering core beliefs so we can compare them to what is true about God. As I considered the assumptions I made from my upbringing, I discovered a couple of recurring messages:

1. Cusses don't ask for help; Cusses help others.
2. Others have it worse. Don't complain.

Interestingly, these two messages are generally true. Our family helps others. My sister is a family attorney who helps people in need of legal protection. I am a pastor. My mother and father both served in clubs that practiced and promoted community service. We're all financially generous to the under-resourced. Cusses help others. What a great trait.

"Others have it worse" is also generally true. My life, compared to many others, is good. What do I have to complain about? This is how our family of origin propagandist can take even positive traits and use them to block our capacity for God's love. If I don't ask for help, and I believe others always have it worse, how will I ever come to God in vulnerability? That is essential in any relationship of love.

Of course, many family of origin propagandists offer much harsher or demeaning messages that cut to our core identity, that cause us to struggle to see ourselves as someone worth loving. Whether what we inherited from our family of origin was positive, negative, or complicated, we can get to the bottom of it. Examine what you're holding and what has taken hold of you and compare it to what is true about the gospel.

If we want to do deeper work, we can look at not just our upbringing but also at the generational traits of our families. "Cusses don't ask for help" goes back at least four generations to my great-grandfather, who homesteaded thousands of acres of land in rugged Australia in the late 1800s. I wrote a chapter in *Managing Leadership Anxiety* about how to make a genogram, which is a tool specifically designed to help us understand generational traits and gain clarity on the family of origin propagandist.

The final committee member we all have in common is our childhood agreements officer. We forge many of our deepest core beliefs in childhood. Children don't have power or agency; they are dependent on adults for that. It is the lack of power and agency that roots these childhood agreements so deep. Kids have core needs such as security, soothing, and safety, but the adults and other children in their lives do not always provide for these needs. Sometimes children's legitimate needs were ignored, causing pain and suffering. In some cases they had to deal with significant and harsh ongoing situations, such as abandonment, horrendous abuse, neglect, and trauma.

A friend of mine was raised by a father who became violent when he was drunk. My friend quickly learned how to appease an angry, drunk father so his siblings and mother would be safe. His childhood skills literally protected him and his family members into adulthood. His agreement was a true life-and-death childhood agreement.

Sometimes agreements are forged by something so small that no one else remembers it except for you. A friend of mine vividly remembers a third-grade teacher placing him in front of the class to make fun of him for his poor test result. His teacher shook his paper in his face and told the class what a bad example he was and that no one should want to be like him. Mortifying! Of course, this was not the teacher's finest moment. But it's possible the teacher does not even remember it. It is also possible that this teacher is actually a decent person. Yet for a boy with no power or agency, that one incident became an infected wound that resulted in an agreement to never appear stupid in public again. That explains why he struggled to speak up in staff meetings as an adult. It also explains why he is a voracious learner.

Humans rub against humans and cause harm, whether they mean to or not, and the sad, painful truth is that some humans mean to cause harm to children. Many of my own childhood agreements were forged from years of being bullied by other children. Those kids absolutely meant me harm, and on a couple of occasions, I thought they would kill me. Sometimes adults do not mean to harm but cause it anyway. Their addictions and struggles harmed their children, even though they deeply loved them. It is the lack of power and agency in a child that roots these agreements so deep in their psyches.

The problem is, we become adults and no longer need these hypervigilant protective mechanisms. But unless we do serious intentional examination, our childhood agreements stay in the arsenal and are easily reactivated. They operate our lives and beliefs. They determine what gets in and out of our hearts. It takes courage to look soberly at these agreements, especially when deeper wounds of violence and neglect are underneath them. That kind of work will often benefit from professional help, from someone such as a skillful therapist. But until you examine these agreements, they will continue to be a primary driver and will often block your capacity to encounter God's love as you depend on self for well-being in those moments rather than on God.

Some may read about these childhood agreements and think, *Come on. No parent or teacher is perfect. Why are you focusing on the negative?* But this journey is not about a parent or a teacher. It is not about looking for someone to blame or finding an affront at every turn. It is about the way we make meaning from pain and lack, and how that meaning forged beliefs that keep us stuck.

I consider myself to be a loving and involved dad, but my kids will be on their own journey of unlocking childhood agreements, looking at moments I may not remember but ones that have created a wound in them.

Dislodging a childhood agreement is difficult because we have been living with ourselves for a long time, and even though it is theologically true that God has been with us too, we did not always experience it as true. So when we faced lack or pain or even abuse as a child, the agreement we may have made was some version of, "You're on your own, kid."

I think the biggest challenge of being human is vulnerably letting God into the deepest parts of our pain when we fear we will be let down or hurt again. Many of us may have looked into these childhood issues, but we have not done the extra step of sifting them through God's Word and God's words. This is where the heart of our faith rests: the forged beliefs that block our faith in God. In my own life, I uncovered some of this task force years ago, but it was not until a decade later that I began to reexamine these dynamics through my faith experience.

We all have an inner critic, a family of origin propagandist, and a childhood agreements officer. Some of us have other committee members, including some vigilant soldiers. At this point, you may feel overwhelmed by all this, but the power of this work isn't in identifying each member; it is gaining clarity on the meaning you make overall and the messages the committee as a whole have reinforced in your life. The work is tackling The Stories We Tell Ourselves and gently challenging The Way Things Are. When we sift them through the heart of the gospel, we can truly experience breakthrough and relief.

SIFTING OUR BELIEFS

Let's get into the core messages. As I considered my own life and my own committee, I discovered these core beliefs that operate my life:

1. God is busy helping those who need it more than me.
2. My problems are not really problems.
3. I must be self-sufficient; I can never be weak or vulnerable.
4. My feelings are not valid; I do not have the rights to them.
5. Strong people figure it out on their own.
6. People must see me as smart for me to be okay and for the world to be okay.
7. God loves me generically, not specifically. God loves me as just another generic person because that is God's job.

It takes work to uncover these specific beliefs, but that is where liberation begins. Now that these beliefs are written in black-and-white,

I can thoughtfully look at them and sift them through the gospel. The list is quite shocking. My brain says there's no way I could actually believe the list, but my actions, my deepest thinking, and my fear offer counterevidence.

As you read the list above, you can see why I struggle to experience God's love. A person can't experience God's love when they minimize their legitimate needs and never come to God with them. They can't experience God's love when they think they don't deserve it, must strive to get it, or do not want to bother God with their minimized problems.

In what ways do you live your life or see the world that keep you from being vulnerable and exposed? Know this, you can't experience God's love if you have Teflon around your heart, deflecting what is trying to get in. You can't count on God to be there if you're convinced that God is unreliable in the face of pain.

This is lifelong work. I still regularly examine all my core beliefs. But you can experience a profound breakthrough by starting with just one. King David wrote in Psalm 139:23–24, "Search me, God, and know my heart; test me and know my anxious thoughts. See if there is any offensive way in me, and lead me in the way everlasting."

Once we have established and clarified our deepest core beliefs, it is time to sift them through our most precious beliefs. The apostle John is helpful as he provides a way to displace our belief about ourselves with what is true about God. In 1 John 3:19–20, John writes, "This is how we know that we belong to the truth and how we set our hearts at rest in his presence: If our hearts condemn us, we know that God is greater than our hearts, and he knows everything."

Our committee members do what they do in order to protect us from hard things and guard us from being hurt when we are vulnerable. They use memory, experiences, and the meaning built from those experiences to keep us safe. The problem is, they simultaneously keep us bound. When we are aware of God's presence, we can get fidgety because it is uncomfortable—even terrifying—to be fully vulnerable and fully exposed before a God who knows everything about us. John uses a phrase in this passage that offers reassurance: "if our hearts condemn us." We condemn ourselves so God or another person cannot condemn us first. John invites us to enter into God's presence so our hearts can fully rest. Our soldiers can stand down and our inner critic can quiet the voice of condemnation. Our hearts are condemning us, but "God is greater than our hearts, and he knows everything."

John invites us to believe what God says about us over and above what we say about ourselves. If we can do that, we can relax into the love of God, letting our guard down and allowing love to seep in. John invites us to let God, not our committee, have the last word. He invites us to dislodge The Stories We Tell Ourselves and The Way Things Are to embrace God's story and God's reality.

This is difficult and ongoing work. Our committee members speak loud and clear, but God often uses a "gentle whisper" (1 Kings 19:12). Our committee members were tangibly present in some early experiences of pain; God's presence is intangible because God is invisible, which is why faith is a key component of experiencing God's love. By faith I embrace God's words over my own words. I change my faith allegiance. I no longer automatically place my faith in the committee in my head, but instead I intentionally place my trust in God. I am not talking about a onetime event where I give my life to God; I am talking about a daily practice. This practice of trusting God over the committee took a few years to establish for me. We have to be patient with ourselves when we walk this path.

Eugene Peterson paraphrases John's words this way: "My dear children, let's not just talk about love; let's practice real love. This is the only way we'll know we're living truly, living in God's reality. It's also the way to shut down debilitating self-criticism, even when there is something to it. For God is greater than our worried hearts and knows more about us than we do ourselves" (1 John 3:18–20 MSG).

THE TANGIBLE LOVE OF GOD

Nowadays, years after I first experienced God's particular love, I have learned to notice it viscerally. I physically relax. My breathing gets deeper and slower. My shoulders unclench. I literally relax into the presence and love of God. This is a habit I practice regularly. I learned to see my body tensing up as a sign that I am moving into a false belief. I pause and locate that belief and then exchange it for what is true about God, and I "remember the Lord."

Exchanging God's reality for ours may not feel tangible enough. It may even feel like a shell game or a "fake it until you make it." But I assure you it is not. The love of God is no less tangible than The Stories We Tell Ourselves; it is just less familiar, so it feels less tangible at first. The stories we believe about ourselves take as much faith as believing in God's love. This practice is simply forcing the issue, placing our life at a fork in the road. *Whom shall I trust? Who gets my heart's deepest allegiance?* Faith is required, no matter what we choose. I am simply suggesting that we all can choose life over self-condemnation. It is much better news. I propose that we place our faith in something more reliable than our own opinions. If we do that long enough, over time God's love will become as tangible as The Stories We Tell Ourselves, and we will discover the story that has been guiding us and speaking to us for decades is not as reliable or true as we assumed it was.

To be honest, I do not place my faith in God's tangible love the majority of the time. Even after years of practice, I am often either oblivious, or I let The Story I Tell Myself committee run on autopilot, pushing me around, keeping me on guard. But when I intentionally engage in this practice—maybe 15 or 20 percent of the time—I experience freedom in Christ, and it is a palpable freedom indeed. It is an experience that truly changes my life. I encourage you to practice it this week.

The next chapter seeks to guide us to practice relaxing into God's love, specifically by learning to quiet our inner critic and think a little more deeply about some of the other committee members in our lives.

DISCUSSION QUESTIONS

1. What committee members are you aware of in your life? Can you name a couple of them specifically?
2. What might be an aspect of The Stories We Tell Ourselves that you would like to examine?
3. What positive message have you inherited that might become a stronghold? (For example, being responsible is a good trait, but always being responsible for everyone's experience is a stronghold.)
4. What negative experiences or messages would you like to explore?
5. Would you like to explore trauma or abuse with the help of a professional? (You can seek out a local church or go to psychologytoday.com and search for "Christian, Trauma," in your city.)
6. If you are ready to do so, list some core beliefs about yourself, the world, or God that might be blocking your capacity to receive God's love.

FOUR

CONTAINING THE INNER CRITIC

For grace to be grace, it must give us things we didn't know we needed and take us places where we didn't want to go.
KATHLEEN NORRIS, *ACEDIA & ME*

You know those inkblot tests where the therapist shows a picture of an inkblot and asks, "What do you see?" You tell the therapist what first comes to mind, and your answer says more about you than it does about the inkblot? The inkblot is intentionally vague—a neutral canvas designed to provoke and reveal our deepest assumptions and biases. Inkblots are a simple way to extract our inner world to be analyzed. The technical name for the inkblot test is the Rorschach test, named after Swiss psychiatrist and psychoanalyst Hermann Rorschach.

Some stories in the Bible serve as a Rorschach test. Bible authors rarely give us insight into what people were thinking and feeling. They focus mostly on actions—what the people they write about were *doing*. We almost never get inside someone's mind to know their inner world, so we often have to imagine our way in. Some incidents don't take much imagination (for example, when King Saul hurled a spear at David or when Joseph turned to weep in private so his brothers wouldn't see him crying). But in most Bible stories, we project thoughts and feelings onto the people. If we pay attention to these projections, we can learn about our assumptions. Remember, assumptions put us in a false reality, and truth sets us free. What if we are projecting onto God something that is not true? What if, like a Rorschach test, the way we interpret biblical characters' inner lives doesn't reflect God's truth as much as it does our own inner worlds—particularly, our inner critics?

Consider Jesus and Peter. When Jesus was on trial for his life in front of Caiaphas and the Sanhedrin, Peter was in the courtyard infamously disowning Jesus in every way imaginable. Jesus had previously predicted that Peter would deny knowing him three times, and Peter was apoplectic. He couldn't fathom such a betrayal of his master and friend. Jesus said Peter would be disloyal, but Peter prided himself on his fierce loyalty. "Even if all fall away on account of you, I never will," he told Jesus in Matthew 26:33. To Peter's credit, he was willing to die for Jesus in Gethsemane when he brandished a sword to protect Jesus from arrest. Jesus and his motley crew were vastly outnumbered by Judas's armed mob. By wielding a sword, Peter was being loyal to Jesus—misguided, yes, but well-intentioned, for sure.

A few short hours later, Peter betrayed his friend by brashly denying over and over even knowing Jesus. Right after Peter's three denials, Jesus was escorted into the courtyard. I'll let Luke take it from here.

> Just as he was speaking, the rooster crowed. The Lord turned and looked straight at Peter. Then Peter remembered the word the Lord had spoken to him: "Before the rooster crows today, you will disown me three times." And he went outside and wept bitterly. (Luke 22:60–62)

That is all we get: "The Lord turned and looked straight at Peter."

Luke offers no indication of Jesus' mood, thinking, or countenance. It isn't hard to imagine what was going through Peter's mind, but what do you think was happening in Jesus' mind when he looked at Peter? Was he angry or disappointed? Was it a "gotcha" look or the knowing look of a parent? Luke doesn't say. When you reflect on Jesus looking straight at Peter, how would you describe Jesus' countenance?

This incident is a Rorschach test. What we see on Jesus' face says more about our view of God than it does about God. It's a way of tuning in to the voice of our inner critic.

I used to see disappointment on Jesus' face. Peter had let Jesus down in one of Jesus' true times of need, so in my projection, Jesus was disappointed and possibly hurt. What I saw on Jesus' face said a lot about my own fear of disappointing Jesus, as well as people in general. I am a chronic people-pleaser who sees disappointment when I look at the face of God. I don't pause to remember that Peter defended Jesus just a few hours before in Gethsemane. When I think about Peter's actions there, I know he messed up, but really, he was trying to follow Jesus the best way he knew how. We don't give Peter enough credit for being willing to lay down his life right then and there.

But back to the courtyard and Jesus fixing his gaze on Peter: What do you see?

I have asked this question to hundreds of people, and the most common answers are "disappointment," "betrayal," "anger," "sadness," and "hurt."

Why don't we look at the face of Jesus and see love and forgiveness? What does it say about me—a lifelong striver and achiever—that I believe in God's unconditional love and God's mercies that are new every morning until I don't perform properly for Jesus, at which point I see disappointment or anger?

What is it about our deepest understanding of God that sees love until we mess up and then sees what we seem to believe are God's true colors? We believe God's unconditional love is skin-deep. But that's not true! God's love flows through the blood in God's veins, right into and out of God's heart. The very center of the universe is a beating heart of love.

You may argue that I am simply substituting one assumption for another with the Rorschach test of Jesus' face. Maybe I am playing fast and loose with this whole Rorschach idea. But we don't have to guess what Jesus' look might have been. The gospel writer John gives us a reasonable indication. Jesus' next encounter with Peter after the courtyard incident took place following the resurrection. Jesus provided a meal for the disciples on the beach, and Peter was overjoyed to see Jesus (see John 21). Jesus had a private conversation with Peter about love and about Peter's unique calling. It was a conversation of restoration and recruitment, forgiveness and mercy. The foundational topic of the chat was love. It was a conversation entirely consistent with what we believe about God's character.

We know Jesus had no filter when it came to frank confrontation with people. If Jesus believed someone needed to be corrected, he did not hesitate to put them in their place. But not this time. Rather than sharing disappointment or anger with Peter, Jesus offered love and restoration.

I'm fascinated that Jesus calls Peter to the very character trait that Peter failed to display in the courtyard—namely, loyalty. The very area where Peter failed Jesus is where Peter will most need to live as he serves Jesus for the rest of his life.

It is difficult to live in the reality of God's unconditional love. We are conditioned to expect that we will cause God to come to the end of God's rope. It takes great faith to overcome our assumptions and live into the vast reality of God's love that stretches farther than the east is from the west. It takes faith to replace our inner critic with the true voice of God's love.

TOOL: CONTAINING THE VOICE OF YOUR INNER CRITIC

One of our most entrenched committee members is our inner critic—the voice that speaks condemnation and shame when we fall short of our own expectations. Work through the following questions to gain some insight into your own inner critic and how it differs from and conflicts with the voice of the Holy Spirit.

Write down some of the messages of your inner critic.

Example: "You should know better by now," in a tone of disappointment. Or, "You're so stupid."

____

____

____

Write down descriptions—adjectives or metaphors—that capture the message of your inner critic.

____

____

____

If you're in a group, capture descriptors for everyone's inner critics.

____

____

____

Take turns reading the list of adjectives to each other.

Read 1 John 3:19–20 in any translation you like, but also in *The Message*.

> This is how we know that we belong to the truth and how we set our hearts at rest in his presence: If our hearts condemn us, we know that God is greater than our hearts, and he knows everything (NIV).

> This is the only way we'll know we're living truly, living in God's reality. It's also the way to shut down debilitating self-criticism, even when there is something to it. For God is greater than our worried hearts and knows more about us than we do ourselves (MSG).

This simple table can help silence the inner critic. When we compare the descriptions of the "gospel" of our inner critic to the true gospel of God, we see the stark contrast.

Living by faith is believing God's words over our words. This is difficult work. You cannot stop your inner critic from coming to work and from speaking, but over time, you can consciously choose to let God have the final word.

What do you think your inner critic needs? How might you invite it to stand down?

____

____

____

Fill in the blank in the following sentence: What if I were at least as __________________________ to myself as God is?

ADJECTIVE COMPARISON	
INNER CRITIC	The Gospel

Pro tip: What is the difference between the voice of our inner critic and the voice of the Holy Spirit? Our inner critic condemns; the Holy Spirit convicts. Our inner critic blames and condemns us at our core identity level; the Holy Spirit addresses our behavior and thoughts. Our inner critic keeps us stuck with no path to redemption; the Holy Spirit offers repentance, repair, forgiveness, and a path to relief.

TOOL: OTHER COMMITTEE MEMBERS

As I mentioned earlier, we do not need to identify each committee member, but the questions and guidance below can help us flesh out the core messages of some of our committee members. Below I point to a way to bring our childhood agreements into the open and a way to understand the assets and liabilities of our family of origin, paying careful attention to the meaning we made from those messages. In each case, the brave and difficult move is to compare them to the gospel of God.

CHILDHOOD AGREEMENTS OFFICER

Childhood agreements can be conscious or unconscious. Their general themes are protection and pain avoidance. We can forge them from one incident, but often they come from a series of incidents. The "single incident" example is my friend whose teacher mocked him in front of the class. A series of incidents might include ongoing bullying or a father's rage.

Childhood agreements can take time to locate. It is okay if you are not ready to try the tools on this page; feel free to come back to them when you are.

Name an event or a series of events that may have generated a childhood agreement.

____

____

____

What agreement did you make with yourself to protect yourself from future harm.

____

____

____

Fill in the blanks in the following sentence that describes a childhood agreement.
I will __________ so that ____________ will never happen again.

Where do you see this agreement keeping you stuck as an adult?

____

____

____

____

Compare your agreement with what is true about God.

____

____

____

____

FAMILY OF ORIGIN PROPAGANDIST

List three or four assumptions or expectations you have inherited from your family of origin.

____

____

____

What are a couple of assets and a couple of liabilities you carry from your family of origin?

____

____

____

What meaning have you made about yourself from those?

____

____

____

What meaning have you made about God from those?

____

____

____

As you compare the meaning you made from your childhood agreements and family of origin with the gospel of God, is it true?

- ☐ Mostly true.
- ☐ Mostly false.
- ☐ Well, it is difficult to make a blanket statement about it.

If you had a traumatic childhood, you . . .

- ☐ . . . are aware, but do not have the capacity to explore it at this time.
- ☐ . . . don't think it is significant enough to explore further.
- ☐ . . . worked on it in the past and may explore it further.
- ☐ . . . will actively seek trauma therapy.

Other unique committee members you are considering:

____

____

____

TOOL: THE FIRST AND FINAL WORD

I am an Australian citizen, which means that King Charles III is my sovereign.

This affects my day-to-day life almost not at all, but if the monarch were to ever summon me to Buckingham Palace, it would be my great honor to go. I know many of my readers prefer to throw perfectly good tea in a harbor and shoot at people wearing red coats, but some of us enjoy being part of the Commonwealth.

A summons from the monarch comes with rules. The king gets the *first* word. You don't just stroll into his presence and start yammering about whatever is on your mind. You wait until he speaks, and then you're permitted to respond. You wouldn't correct the king. Can you imagine mansplaining to the king?

The king also gets the *final* word. He decides when he's done with the meeting.

The king gets the first word and the final word.

For followers of Christ, God is our sovereign King, but too often we let our inner critic get the first and final word. It takes faith and practice to live in such a way that God has the first and final word in our lives.

For a couple of years, I tried to stop my inner critic from speaking. I tried to fire it one time, but the next day it still showed up to work. That is the insidious nature of the committee—if we try to completely eliminate them, they go on even higher alert. I have learned a better way. Now I let my inner critic say its piece, but I no longer give it the final word. And after some reps with that, I try to live in such a way that I do not let it have the first word either. I do not eliminate my inner critic's voice; I contain it with the truth of God.

One of the reasons we struggle to encounter God's love is because we give our inner critic, The Stories We Tell Ourselves, the first and the final word. We give more weight to what we say than what God says.

God says we are "fearfully and wonderfully made" (Psalm 139:14) and that "even the very hairs of your head are all numbered" (Matthew 10:30). God's love for us is *particular* and *specific*. We are known and seen and loved. But our inner critic says, "If people really knew who I am . . ."

God says, "Therefore, there is now no condemnation for those who are in Christ Jesus" (Romans 8:1). But our inner critic continues to condemn us. Some of us even encourage this sickness in the name of humility. We focus on, "Do not think of yourself more highly than you ought" (Romans 12:3) and, "Value others above yourselves"

(Philippians 2:3), but frankly, most of us hold the opposite problem. As Rick Warren wrote in *The Purpose Driven Life*, "Humility is not thinking less of yourself; it is thinking of yourself less."[1]

There is nothing humble about placing our opinion of ourselves over God's opinion. That isn't humility; it is old-fashioned arrogance.

So lately, I've been living by faith—faith that God knows better than me. God's first and final words orient my days. My inner critic still yammers, and I let it say its piece, but once the word has been spoken, I intentionally frame its word between God's good words.

THE FIRST AND FINAL WORD IS *LIFE*

When God speaks first, amazing things happen. In Genesis 1, God speaks, and life starts flowing. Life upon life upon life, everywhere you look, from the Venus flytrap to the giraffe to God's image bearers. I love how the author of Genesis describes the life that flows in the waters of the early creation festival: it "teems" (Genesis 1:20–21). I have had the pleasure of scuba diving a handful of times, and *teeming* is the perfect word for all the life happening in the ocean. When God speaks first, life teems forth.

God also has the first word in John 1. He describes a new creation. We can begin to see why John intentionally cut and pasted the first few words from Genesis when he started his gospel. "In the beginning . . ." triggers our memories of the first "In the beginning," with all the wonder of creation that poured out of God's first word. John reminds us that God's first word is stunning. In this case, God's word "became flesh and made his dwelling among us" (verse 14). Every Advent and Christmas season, we approach a backwoods manger with anticipation and great wonder at the life that showed up: Immanuel, God with us.

---

1. Rick Warren, *The Purpose Driven Life: What on Earth Am I Here For?* (Grand Rapids: Zondervan, 2002), 148.

Even after Jesus died and was buried in a garden tomb, God's word was living and active, "sharper than any double-edged sword (Hebrews 4:12). On Resurrection Sunday morning, Mary Magdalene saw Jesus but mistook him for a gardener. I wonder if John's sense of humor is shining through, or if he is still connecting us back to Genesis. Jesus had toiled hard for five metaphorical days, teaching and healing and challenging the religious establishment. On the sixth day came his pinnacle creation: dying on the cross for humanity. On the seventh day he rested in the tomb. And now the first day—a new creation. No wonder Mary thought he was the gardener; he was cultivating a garden 2.0. He still is. "For where two or three gather in my name, there am I with them" (Matthew 18:20). The new garden does not require Utopia; it just requires Jesus' presence because Jesus is "the way and the truth and the life" (John 14:6). A new garden on earth as it is in heaven.

God's first word is *life*.

God has a final word as well. As a pastor, I have officiated a lot of funerals. Being around death is an occupational hazard. Death steals. Death does not negotiate. It is absolute.

Death is arrogant. Have you ever met someone who has to have the last word in every discussion? You tell a story, and they have to tell a better story. It can feel like death does that. It acts like a one-upper. We're often struck dumb by the power of death, reeling in its wake. It leaves while we are still trying to catch our breath, so it's sure it has the final word.

But we do not grieve like people who have no hope (see 1 Thessalonians 4:13). We are not uninformed. God is King, not death. God is supreme, not death. Once death has finished running its mouth, saying all it has to say, wreaking havoc, stealing, and destroying, God speaks. God ends the conversation with a final word: *life. Resurrection*.

Made. New.

God's first word is *life*; God's final word is *life*.

"Death, be not proud," says John Donne, "though some have

called thee mighty and dreadful, for thou art not so. . . . Death, thou shalt die." At the end of all things, death will be cast out, consumed in the lake of fire. All that will be left is life.

In the dark moments of my faith, when I am feeling swallowed up by doubt, when I encounter evil firsthand, when a friend faces tragic loss, I am comforted by remembering God's first and final word. Often when I lose sight of God, it is because I feel the pressure to take action, but in those moments, I try to remember that my job is to notice God at work and then to join God in that action. God's first word, then my response, then God's final word.

I can do that.

DISCUSSION QUESTIONS

1. In the Rorschach test of Jesus looking at Peter after his denial, what did you see on Jesus' face?
2. As you listen to others share their view about Jesus' approach to Peter, what is your response to them?
3. How is it that we can see the falsehood in someone else's inner critic but allow our own inner critic to run our brain unchallenged?
4. What adjectives and descriptions did you write down as others shared their inner critic's messages?
5. How do those adjectives compare to the ways you would describe the gospel of Jesus?
6. We pointed out other task force members (such as the family of origin propagandist and the childhood agreements officer). What messages have you embraced from them?
7. Are there any other task force members you would like to explore?
8. What practice this week can help you live into God's first and final word?

FIVE

GAP 2: GOD'S VISCERAL PRESENCE

"I Believe God Is with Me, but I Don't See Him"

Everything I've ever let go of has claw marks on it.
DAVID FOSTER WALLACE, *INFINITE JEST*

I enjoy television shows and movies that use an unreliable narrator. An unreliable narrator is exactly like it sounds—the voice in a story that tells us what's going on is giving false or misleading information. We implicitly trust a narrator because their job is to help orient us to what is happening, which makes an *unreliable* narrator such a devious and engaging technique for telling a story.

Probably the most well-known unreliable narrator in modern movies is Bruce Willis in *The Sixth Sense*. We oriented to the story through his point of view. Of course, he wasn't intentionally deceiving us. He was as confused as we were, but the screenwriter used him as an unreliable narrator to create intrigue. Many movies like *The Sting*, *The Prestige*, and *Memento*, as well as television shows like *Homeland* use various forms of an unreliable narrator to confuse an audience with what should be a trustworthy source of information. We implicitly trust the narrator but discover over the course of the story that we were misled.

You and I have a narrator in our lives. It tells us what we need, and it prompts us to get those things. This can be as simple as, "You need to eat," or "You need to sleep," and as complicated as, "You need this person to like you," or "You need to do this perfectly; here is how you could have done the last project better." Sometimes the narrator is quite powerful and can block external inputs, so when someone compliments you, the narrator says, "Don't trust that person; you know you are not that good." Of course, we do not audibly hear the narrator speaking. It works more like an instinct. It speaks subconsciously, moving us around to get our needs. Most of the time, it acts like an autopilot. Occasionally we take the rudder, but generally we trust the narrator to fly us right. Our life narrator uses a mix of thinking, breathing, hormones, and chemicals to keep us alive and thriving in the story of our lives. The problem is, we have two kinds of needs, true needs and false needs, and our narrator cannot always tell the difference. It uses the same mix of thinking, breathing, hormones, and chemicals to go after our true needs and our false needs, and this is where things become problematic.

When we do not get our needs met, our narrator warns us that we are in danger. If we do not eat or if we neglect sleep or if our child goes missing on the playground, our narrator alerts us, and we move to get what we need. We eat; we sleep; we drop everything to look for our child. In those situations, our narrator is reliable and helpful, keeping us and our loved ones alive, safe, and thriving.

But our narrator also alerts us to danger in circumstances that are not dangerous at all. This happens when we do not get our false needs met. False needs are pesky. When we look at them soberly, we know they are false, but in the moment, our narrator is awfully convincing that they are true needs and that we are in danger if we don't acquire them. Often, our narrator wildly exaggerates about what will happen if we don't meet a false need. It alerts us that, "Armageddon is about to happen!"

For the same reasons I love unreliable narrators in movies, I hate the unreliable narrator in my head. Misdirection and tension are great in films, but they're terrible in real life. I am surprised at how surly and persistent the unreliable narrator in my own life is. Unreliable narrators are one reason why we stay in stuck patterns for years. For example, right now I can soberly tell you that I do not need everyone's approval, but when I am in front of someone who disapproves of me, my unreliable narrator sets off alarms. Right now I can tell you that when someone is venting about their problems, they do not need my advice to make them feel better, but in the moment that's happening, my narrator becomes wildly unreliable. It tells me I need to tell that person what to do with their life. My narrator cannot tell the difference between someone venting and my own need to intervene, someone's need and my need to be needed.

If you are a perfectionist, your unreliable narrator wildly exaggerates what will happen if you make a mistake. Consider what would happen if you sent out an official email with three grammatical errors in it. In reality, very little would happen. Maybe someone would point out the errors, but more likely, no one would ever say anything—and many people wouldn't notice! But if you are a perfectionist, even as you read this you are having a reaction in your body. You might be shuddering just thinking about it. That is your unreliable narrator claiming you are in danger. You actually are not. It believes leaving grammatical errors in an email will put you in danger. That is not true. It turns out your need for perfection is a *false* need because you can thrive as a human without it. One way you can measure your unreliable narrator is to notice how it exaggerates the stakes if you do not get your false need.

THE "BIG 5" FALSE NEEDS

I have taught thousands of people to locate their false needs, and we always begin by looking at the "Big 5" false needs of every human. They are control, perfection, knowing the answer, being there for people, and approval. As we look at these one at a time, we may find that we relate to some or maybe even all of them.

CONTROL

Some people are control freaks. They walk into a meeting and have already thought through six possible scenarios that people will raise in that meeting. If someone raises a scenario they haven't anticipated, they get defensive or combative, not because the person raised a lousy issue, but because they were caught unprepared. When they go out to eat with a group of friends and someone suggests a restaurant they know will be a bad experience, they use their strong personality to shift the vote of the group. But they justify it because it is, they say, for the greater good.

They need their people to behave in a certain way so they can relax. When they host a meeting and Jim is going on and on without an end in sight, they get anxious because they set up the meeting and don't want Jim's actions to reflect poorly on them. When they don't get their false need of control met, they respond poorly.

PERFECTION

As discussed earlier, some people are perfectionists who believe they must get everything right the first time, even though they may have never done the task before. When they look at their work, they don't say, "That was well done." Instead they say, "Here is how I could have done it better." If someone compliments them, they either correct them to their face or politely smile and say thank you, even though they disagree with what the person is saying. They got an A on a project, but in their heart, they know it was really a B-. The concept of good enough is anathema. A preventable mistake is a venial sin, possibly a mortal one. When someone offers them feedback on their work, they intercept them by listing everything wrong with it first. They need others to know that they know they can do it better. They never relax into being human-sized. They believe God wants them to strive for perfection, even though they will never get there.

KNOWING THE ANSWER

Some of us need to always be the one with the right answer. This is one of my struggles. If I am in a meeting and Jimmy asks Renae a question, I feel compelled to answer, even though Jimmy didn't ask me the question. If I know something, I need you to know that I know. When a telemarketer calls, telling me their records show that my vehicle warranty is about to expire, and I know they don't have a file of my vehicles, I try to make them confess that they don't know what vehicles I own. I then try to explain that I can't trust someone to sell me a warranty when they are so deceptive. Why not just say "no thanks" and hang up the phone? I have an incessant need to prove that I cannot be fooled and that I am not stupid.

Nowadays, when the phone rings, a robot is typically on the other end of the line. And these robots are getting really good at sounding like interactive humans. They can listen to my answers to their questions and then give a recorded response as though we're having a proper human conversation. When I suspect I am talking to a robot, I will ask what its favorite color is to prove to the robot that I know it is a robot. At the end of the call, I am all smug that I was right, and my wife looks at me as if to say, "You wasted three minutes proving a robot isn't a human. Congratulations." But I consider that to be time well spent. It is certainly better than anyone ever thinking I am stupid, even a robot. Being seen as stupid is the worst.

Maybe you are like me, and you are an incessant researcher. You are a human Google. You are happy to look something up for someone rather than letting them learn it on their own. You love to teach. The three most painful words in the English language for you are "I don't know."

BEING THERE FOR PEOPLE

Some people need to be there for others who are hurting. I can relate to this as well. My brain struggles to discern the difference between someone else's need and my incessant need to be needed. When someone is venting to me about a problem, my brain tells me, "They want your advice," or "They want you to swoop in and save the day." If you are like me, when someone is suffering, you cannot sit by, even though you may already be overcommitted with helping others. If two friends are at odds with each other, we anxiously try to intervene because we are not okay when they are not okay. Maybe we overcommit to help and then cannot keep all our commitments, and rather than see ourselves as the problem, we blame others for not helping too. Why is it that those of us who love to be there for others often feel lonely? We are always checking in on people, but who is checking on us? The truth is, our friends gave up checking in on us long ago because every time they asked how we were doing, we answered, "I'm fine." We help others, but we struggle to ask others for help.

APPROVAL

Some of us crave other people's approval. If we disappoint someone or perceive that someone does not like us, we can get quite anxious. Maybe we walk away from a conversation and incessantly replay it, evaluating how we came across. We spend too much of our time living in someone else's brain. *What are they thinking? What do they think of me?* Perhaps we believe that if someone misunderstands us or misattributes our motives, we can convince them with more words. Even though many people enjoy our company, we focus on the few who do not. *If only they could see my heart, they would know I am a good person.* Disrespect is a huge trigger, and we respond with quick anger.

People who need approval often need more external validation than they receive, so they brag in subtle ways, looking for a pat on the head. Their inner life is defined by the need for validation.

Where do you find yourself in the Big 5? Perhaps you look at this list and think, *I'm doomed. I am all five.* If you see yourself in all five, take heart. It will be fine. You can be free. Your first step is to discern which of the Big 5 is *foundational* for you. For me, even though I have three of the five, my foundational false need is *approval.* I like to have the answer and I like to be there for people so I can get approval.

ACUTE AND CHRONIC ANXIETY

Detangling true needs from false needs can be difficult but fruitful work, and it begins by locating ourselves in the Big 5. Technically what we are doing is detangling our acute anxiety from our chronic anxiety. Acute anxiety shows up when we have a true need that is not being filled, mostly related to physical health and safety. When we or one of our loved ones are in danger, acute anxiety shows up, along with its helpful friend adrenaline, to get our keisters moving. Chronic anxiety is sneakier. It shows up and acts like acute anxiety in situations where we are not in danger. The problem is, our narrator struggles to know the difference.

Chronic anxiety is insidious in nature. It is based on false need. But in the moment, the need is very convincing. It is so convincing that we do not even think about it; we just accept it as true. When someone is disappointed in me or critical of me, when my people are in conflict with one another, or when I do not know the answer and feel stupid and exposed, my narrator becomes highly unreliable and tells me I am under threat. In that moment, I get filled with reactivity.

Sadly, my body gets used to that feeling. Acute anxiety is easier to spot because it comes on so quickly, accompanied by a huge dose of adrenaline and a rapid heart rate. It is usually associated with something visible, like a swerving car or a snake on a jogging path. But chronic anxiety provides a slow, steady drip, drip, drip of activated hormones that keep us on low-grade alert. Chronic anxiety is also difficult because it is typically based on something intangible. It shows up when someone gives us a bemused look, when we make a mistake in public, or when things go south in a meeting. Have you ever had trouble switching off your worry brain? Or have you noticed your heart racing because of a relationship, not because of a car accident? Or have you suddenly noticed that you're carrying all your stress in your shoulders or stomach? That is chronic anxiety.

Chronic anxiety does not dissipate on its own; it has to be displaced. But if we do not even know we have it, it just keeps building, which can lead to exhaustion and burnout—not because of too much work, but because of too much unaddressed chronic anxiety.

THE FIRST TEMPTATION

If we consider the Big 5—that is, the five core false needs of every human—we discover two interesting traits. The first is that each false need is a giant carrot dangling forever out of reach. We will never be in control; we will never do it perfectly; we will never know all there is to know; we will never be there for everyone in need; and we will never get everyone we ever meet to like us. These are impossible goals. They are pots of gold at the end of the rainbow we are chasing. Our chronic anxiety pushes us to strive for something we can never attain.

The second trait is that the five core false needs are five core traits of God's character. God is in control; God is perfect; God knows everything; God is there for everyone; and God gives us approval through his work, not through our striving. These five traits are why God is God and we are not. We strive toward something we will never reach and something we were never designed to have.

In the Garden of Eden, the first temptation the Accuser offered to Adam and Eve was, "You can be like God." We have been falling for that offer ever since. It is difficult to notice God when we are trying to be like God. Our unreliable narrators have us temporarily living in an illusion, operating out of reactivity rather than connected presence. God exists in reality, so when we are in an illusion, it is difficult to see God. It is especially difficult to notice God when we have overreached as humans and try to do God's job for God.

If we pay close attention, we may even discover a more alarming truth: We are doing God's job because we believe God is asleep at the wheel or not up to the task. We take matters into our own hands. It is ironic, isn't it? We strive for control or perfection—or whatever Big 5 need we chase—and we never get it. Perfectionists, when was the last time you looked at your work and said, "That was *perfect*." Probably never. We never attain the thing we believe we need, yet we keep striving. All the while, God invites us to relax into being human-sized. God invites us to trust God to do God's job and us to do a human-sized job. Somewhere along the way, we subconsciously or knowingly decided God wasn't doing enough. Maybe we felt that God let us down, and on some level we said, "I'll take it from here."

You may wonder what exactly is a "human-sized" job? If control, perfection, always knowing the answer, and so forth are God-sized, then what are we to do? Shall we just relax into laziness and indifference? Not at all. Each of the Big 5 has a human-sized equivalent. For example, control freaks are great at attending to detail to ensure that people will have a good experience. Gifted event planners are the kind of people who can be prone to control. I recently spoke at an event that took place in a hotel conference room. The organizer noticed that there were very few power outlets, so she ran extension cords to every table with a power strip on top so people could charge their devices. She taped down the cords so no one would trip. When people walked in, they could immediately plug in their devices at their seat. Now that is a gifted event planner who wants to maximize everyone's experience. That is next-level thoughtfulness and attention to detail. That is human-sized.

But if the organizer spends the whole workshop anxiously noticing who isn't engaged and who looks bored and what she needs to do to guarantee a good time, that is "overfunctioning." Now she has crossed over into control. Ensuring everyone has power at their table—that is human-sized and something she is capable of doing. Worrying about whether people are having a good time—now she has crossed into something she can never have, which is control. She has moved into God's domain.

The difference can feel subtle, but there is in fact a canyon-sized gap between a human-sized effort and a God-sized one, and it usually comes down to overfunctioning and never hitting a target. Perfectionists are gifted at improving things and are very meticulous and careful. Those who need to know the answer are often gifted teachers; they love to research. Those who need to be needed are often very caring and thoughtful. People who struggle with approval are often kind and courteous.

Our Big 5 false needs are typically the twisted extremes of our gifting. God has gifted and wired each of us to make a human-sized contribution to his kingdom, but we tend to twist those gifts into extreme versions. Over time, we can begin to cross over from operating out of our gifting into needing something we can never attain. We feel ourselves pursuing our false needs.

God is God; we are human. Anytime we try to carry more than God designed us to carry, we become filled with chronic anxiety. Anytime we do not get what we believe we need in order to be okay, we become reactive. Reactivity starts small but rapidly expands to take over every nook and cranny of our souls, pushing out the spaces where we notice God. This is why most people do not know they are anxious until they experience an extreme level of anxiety. If you think about the last time you were filled with reactivity, you probably felt a sense of doom or dread or an idea that everything rested on your shoulders, that you must *do something*. Maybe you kept ruminating to figure it out, trying to worry your way to peace. Your awareness of God was displaced because you were trying to do a God-sized task.

Let's look at this theologically for a moment. This habit of seeking false needs and depending on ourselves is self-righteousness. When we first think of the term *self-righteousness*, we think of superiority, as if we consider ourselves to be better than other people. But true self-righteousness can simply be depending on ourselves to be righteous. In this case, *righteous* doesn't mean "correct" or "superior"; it means "well." When the Bible refers to a person as righteous, it describes someone who is well—well with God, well with themselves, and well with others. We all want to be well, but we often depend on ourselves to be well. In those moments when we are not depending on God to make us well, we struggle to relax into God's presence. And this keeps us stuck and spinning. Self-righteousness is the fundamental reason we struggle to notice God.

God presents us with a remarkable offer. We can be well as we depend on God for our righteousness rather than on ourselves. We are prone to shortchange God's righteousness, mostly associating it with God's holiness or Jesus' death on the cross for our sin. Of course, it includes those things. Sin makes us sick, and God heals us of our sin infection. But this new wellness can define not just our eternal destiny, but also our day-to-day reality. We can relax into God's righteousness every day by giving ourselves permission to be exactly human-sized, which is all that God ever expects from us. Remember that only God is God-sized. When we pause and focus on who God is and who we are in God, we relax and start worshiping.

What might this approach look like? It starts with clarity on the division of labor. What is God's job and what is our job? Between us and God, only one of us is surprised that we are exactly human-sized.

God is in control, so I don't have to be. God is perfect; I can do it well enough. God knows it all; I can be curious. God is there for everyone; I do not need to save the day. God frees me from needing human approval because of the grace of unconditional love.

When I plant these truths in my heart, I begin to know what "relaxing into God's presence" means. When I pause and recognize that I am carrying more than God asks me to carry or that I have invaded territory that belongs to God, I can "remember the Lord" and exchange burdens. My soul breathes, and I open up to the possibility of God's presence in that moment.

Jesus died, so I don't have to ______________ anymore.

Jesus died to free me from needing ____________ anymore.

What words or phrases fill those blanks for you?

You may be concerned that I'm advocating for a selfish faith that doesn't connect to the pain and problems of this world, as though all this inner work results in daily hangouts in God's hot tub. You may be concerned that I support indifference to the massive suffering in this world. "So long as we are well, who cares about anyone else?" In fact, the opposite is true. When human-sized humans partner with a God-sized God, we can enter into those broken and evil places with a deeper capacity to do the difficult work because we are actively joining in God's work, not striving to do it on our own.

When I was a chaplain, I sometimes did marathon shifts—twenty-eight hours in a row. Some of those days brought an onslaught of death and pain. I was surprised to learn that my capacity to enter into pain and difficulty massively increased when I relaxed into God's presence. It was as if, for the first time, I could live into these words from the apostle Paul: "I can do everything through Christ, who gives me strength" (Philippians 4:13 NLT). How? By no longer relying on my own strength or trying to be more than God had made me to be. The more I accepted my humanity, the more I saw the wonder of God's power and presence.

This approach is counterintuitive, but it works because we enter those difficult places with lowered reactivity and an increased awareness of God's presence and work. I have consulted with many Christian organizations that are on the front lines of grinding poverty and evil—global child advocacy, foster care, and anti-sex-slavery organizations. My experience is that the more intense the work, the more vital it is to get clarity on this division of labor, and the more I have to intentionally practice relaxing into God's presence. Otherwise I won't make it. I will burn out, become jaded, or slip into a messiah complex, believing it is all on me.

When I try to be like Christ, I always fall short. Then when I apply a more-of-the-same mentality, I end up in a spin cycle of anxiety. In contrast, when I focus on dying to self and remember that God has folded my life into the righteousness of Christ, I relax. God then animates me by God's Spirit, forming and forging me as a human. God's job is to be God; my job is to follow Jesus, die to self, and worship God. That is a job I can do. That is an easy burden and a light yoke.

DYING TO SELF

The apostle Paul talks a lot about dying to self. In his stunning letter to the Colossians, he writes, "For you died, and your life is now hidden with Christ in God" (3:3). I find so much comfort in that simple verse. I die, and my life is now hidden with Christ in God. I picture no longer being alone and exposed, but tucked under God's wing, alongside Jesus. In that position, I can co-labor with God.

What does dying to self look like? The most tangible way I know to die to self is to be hyperaware of the Big 5 and my false needs. These are all signals that I am depending on self. The Big 5 help me locate the specific areas where I have fallen into living for self instead of dying to self. Another signal is my reactivity level. I have learned to notice when my reactivity is increasing, and rather than being flooded by it, I try to pause and remember the Lord. The final signal is that I no longer notice God's presence. How do you become aware that you've stopped noticing God? It takes intentional reminders and often becomes apparent only in retrospect.

Because I am human, I spend most of my life depending on myself. I teach these tools and have practiced them for years, but the fact remains that I am still exactly human-sized. I get anxious; I strive for more; I give into my false needs most of the time. As I became more intentional about these tools, the most surprising revelation was that when I relax into God's presence—even 10 to 15 percent of the time—I feel utterly free. It is as if that little gain or little win with God gives me a massive boost in my faith and well-being. This will be especially difficult for anyone who is a perfectionist. Rather than going for 100 percent, set your first goal at 5 percent. Can you intentionally practice this 5 percent more this week? Transformation is slow and steady, and you and I will ever and always be human.

This practice has the benefit of lowering my threshold to worship. Since the Big 5 are God's core character traits, they are also the reasons I worship God, so when I am no longer striving for them, I am correctly oriented as a human around God, who is in control, perfect, and so on. When I get off the anxiety treadmill, pause, and reflect on who God is and who I am in God, my heart fills with gratitude, and worship naturally pours out of me.

It's especially difficult to notice when I have stopped noticing God. I either go through my day doing, doing, doing or I am so busy striving for what I cannot have that I forget the Lord. I have found two habits helpful in cultivating my awareness of God. The first habit is to know my triggers and false pursuits and lower my threshold of awareness for them.

It is too difficult a leap to go straight from being reactive to noticing God in the moment. The essential baby step is to spend time reflecting back on recent times when we were reactive, when we did not notice God's presence. Even now you can pause and reflect back on a recent time when you forgot God was with you, felt it was all on you, and pushed through with your own strength to sort it out.

Does a situation come to mind, or are you like me, where seven dozen situations come to mind? Good. Next, are any of those situations recurring? Do you often find yourself in similar situations that keep you triggered and unaware of God? Now you are reflecting not on one incident but on a pattern of behavior.

One simple example for me is my preaching. For the first seven years of being a lead pastor, I put myself under intense pressure to preach well. After I preached, I would immediately begin to feel the pressure for the next week. My preaching was connected to three of the Big 5: knowing the answer, being there for people, and seeking people's approval. I would pray as part of my preparation for the sermon during the week, but as I walked out to preach and in the hours after I preached I was more reactive than normal. I was unaware of God's presence. I had to learn to pause, get off the reactivity treadmill, and remember that God is with me, that I am not alone, and that the burdens are not all on my shoulders.

The second habit is to practice pausing in the moment and remembering the Lord. I focus on two specific truths: (1) God is with me right now, and (2) God is already ahead of me, at work in the situation about which I am anxious. So as I walked out to preach, filled with the adrenaline and fear that come with public speaking on behalf of God, I paused to remember the Lord. As I walked over to the music stand and placed my iPad on it, I remembered that God is not only with me, but God is already ahead of me, sovereign and at work in the space I was entering. *This sermon is not on me. I am partnering with the God who is already working in people's hearts.* I repeat this "God with me, God already ahead of me" phrase for any situation in my life that I know will generate anxiety. It isn't difficult. It just takes intentionality.

DISCUSSION QUESTIONS

1. Which of the Big 5 are you most prone to: control, perfection, knowing the answer, being there for people, or approval?
2. Can you recall a recent time when you succumbed to one of the Big 5? What happened?
3. What is an unreliable narration in your life that can get you into trouble?
   - Jesus died, so I don't have to ________ anymore. What words or phrases would you use to fill in the blank for you?
   - Jesus died to free me from needing _______ anymore. What words or phrases would you use to fill in the blank for you?
4. What are some signs that alert you to the times when you stopped noticing God?

SIX

ADDRESSING CHRONIC ANXIETY

Believing takes practice.
MADELEINE L'ENGLE, *A WRINKLE IN TIME*

I live in the Denver metro area, which is infamous for being highly unchurched. As a result, we attract church planters like blood attracts sharks. I like that. We need more effective churches to reach people here. Unfortunately, we also attract young, energetic church planters with a lot of hubris. This is a complex situation because some hubris and youthful energy are necessary to plant a church in the first place. But hubris often masks false needs—control, perfection, and more. And wherever false needs are being chased, chronic anxiety is sure to be lurking.

I occasionally get a flyer in my mailbox advertising a new church coming to town. One day, I pulled out a flyer about a church plant led by a pastor from the Midwest. On the flyer, underneath the name of the church, was the caption, "Bringing God to the Front Range of Denver"—a new church setting out to bring God from a section of the Bible Belt, USA, where apparently God previously lived.

When the young church planter came to town for preparation meetings, a couple of us pastors took him out for lunch. We told him that renowned author Philip Yancey moved to the Denver area in the late 1990s, so God had been in Denver at least since then! We explained to this well-intentioned church planter that he wasn't "bringing God" anywhere, but that if he would like to join God in the work God was already doing—and had been doing for eons before we showed up and would continue to do long after we are gone—then we would eagerly welcome him to join all of us.

We wanted to not only reframe the church planter's hubris and presumption, but also to help him relax. Church planting has enough pressure without the anxiety and weightiness of bringing God into a new territory. Who could ever do that? But all of us can learn to notice God as we enter spaces, recognizing that God got there ahead of us and is already at work.

We can all become a small piece of God's grand story. That is how I survived chaplaincy and the onslaught of death and trauma every day. Death and trauma took me to the end of myself quicker than any other context, and I would quickly get tired or irritable. A chaplain's job is to represent the peace of Christ in the worst moments of people's lives, so I used to think I was bringing Christ into a room. But of course, Christ is always with the brokenhearted, so he beat me there by a wide margin. When I walked into that room of grief, fear, and death, I asked God to attend to my own fearful heart and my own need to say something or do something to make everything all better. I was joining in God's existing work, co-laboring with God. I did that day after day after day. I still grew weary, of course, but my capacity to serve people expanded because I remembered that God was already at work. Jesus' burden is, in fact, light and his yoke is easy. We can all do that.

TOOL: GOD WITH ME, GOD AHEAD OF ME

How do we cultivate a habit of noticing that God is with us and ahead of us? Below is a step-by-step process to consider trying.

Prework: Make a small list of signs or signals that you are forgetting the Lord's presence. These signals are usually related to your reactivity, so you can begin by asking, *How do I know when I am reactive?*

For me, the signals are:

- worrying my way to peace
- low-grade rumination, thinking harder but never resolving anything
- self-pity or indignation, such as when I feel a need for people to know how hard my situation is
- anger or arrogance, such as when I feel a need to put someone in their place on social media
- the desire to escape and watch television
- a tendency to exaggerate my situation

Of course, the signs can be different, depending on the situation at hand, but the preliminary work is learning to notice the recurring signals that you are filled with chronic anxiety and no longer noticing God. If you can learn to notice these postures, they can become an invitation to pause and "remember the Lord."

Once you have done your prework and are armed with information about your triggers, you can try noticing them this week. Once you have noticed a trigger, you can proceed through the following steps:

STEP 1: PAUSE. Take a moment to reflect on yourself and write down any signals that reveal that you have forgotten God. Just pausing to reflect can change the power dynamic with chronic anxiety, which wants you to keep going, keep running on that treadmill to nowhere. Now that you've paused to reflect, you're ready for step two.

STEP 2: REMEMBER THAT GOD IS WITH YOU. Before I walked into a room fresh with the experience of death and grief, I paused to remember that God was with me—that I was not alone—and that my ministry responsibilities were not all on my shoulders. This act of remembering helps me relax into God's presence. In situations that generate anxiety in me, this tool also helps me lower my frustration or irritation with some people. If I have a meeting coming up with a difficult person, I pause and reflect that *God is with me, God is ahead of me.* I also remember that God is with them. It is difficult to remain irritated at someone with whom God is present. Sometimes I pause and remember that 100 percent of the *imago Dei* resides in the person. That thought helps ensure that I treat them with dignity and respect. I work on listening to learn rather than listening to defend. I do not do this because I am the better person; I do it to be free from irritation and from the need to be right.

STEP 3: REMEMBER THAT GOD IS AHEAD OF YOU. God is already working in the space about which you are anxious. As I walked into the room of death and grief, I remembered that I was not bringing God into that room with me but was entering a space where God was sovereign and already at work. I was able to relax into God's presence because it was not on me to do or say anything. My job was to be present to God and present to the people in the room. I felt the weight lift off my shoulders as I realized this. Perhaps this kind of knowledge was how Paul could write, "I can do all this through him who gives me strength" (Philippians 4:13).

STEP 4: LEAVE THE RESULTS TO GOD. As I considered my preaching and the amount of chronic anxiety it produced in me, I learned to relax into God's presence by leaving the results to God. As a pastor, I follow a strict sermon preparation routine that typically takes between twelve and sixteen hours a week. The preparation involves several readings of the Scripture passage, doing commentary research, editing the structure of the message, and so on. I learned to relax into God's presence by measuring my success by my preparation. *Have I done the work? Have I followed the steps and put in the time?* If so, then as I walk out to preach, entering a space where God is already at work, I offer what I have and leave the outcome to God. Simply shifting the success of the sermon from my own unreliable opinion to my preparation was a game changer for me. I offer this example to help you grab hold of the carrot dangling out there that is making you anxious.

STEP 5: USE THIS TOOL PROACTIVELY. Get out your calendar and find an appointment in the next week or two that you know will generate anxiety for you. Open that event and set an alarm so your phone flashes a reminder of the event ten to sixty minutes before the meeting. Now edit the name of the event and add the words, in all caps, "GOD WITH US, GOD AHEAD OF US." So if the original meeting was, "Meet with Jim," now it will say, "GOD WITH US, GOD AHEAD OF US. Meet with Jim."

And ten to sixty minutes before the meeting, your phone will remind you to pause and remember the Lord.

TOOL: ANXIETY, FREEDOM, AND THE GOSPEL

When it comes to God being God and me being human, I use a comparison table to clarify what I can do and what only God can do. As I wrote earlier, the Big 5 are simply the gifts and talents God has given us, twisted and distorted into an idol we cannot attain. An important aspect of getting off the Big 5 treadmill is paying attention to the impact it has on us and our people.

Each of the Big 5 comes with a God-sized job, a human-sized equivalent that we can all do and manage, and an impact or price. Supply your own ideas in the table.

Take special notice of the third column. Many of us stay stuck in the Big 5 striving because we never pause to consider the damage it does to us and others. The Big 5 are like power tools best left in the all-powerful, all-loving hands of God. When we take up a chainsaw, we can easily cause damage. By recognizing the damage and its impacts, we can more clearly see that we need to relax into being human-sized.

	GOD-SIZED JOB	HUMAN-SIZED JOB	IMPACT ON ME AND OTHER PEOPLE WHEN I TRY TO DO GOD'S JOB
CONTROL			
PERFECTION			
KNOWING THE ANSWER			
BEING THERE FOR PEOPLE			
APPROVAL			

This week, I will notice when I am striving for any of the Big 5:

- ☐ Control
- ☐ Perfection
- ☐ Knowing the answer
- ☐ Being there for people
- ☐ Approval

And I will endeavor to notice it and die to it by:

____

____

____

____

Another simple tool is to think about a specific situation, relationship, or project we are anxious about. Often we get anxious not only because we are doing God's job but also because we are worrying about another person. The simplest example is if we have someone in our life who is struggling, which leads to worrying our way to their peace. Or perhaps they are frustrating us, and we are ruminating about why they do what they do. We are trying to change them by thought alone. Changing people is God's territory.

The table above is for general categories, but the questions below are to help us get clear on specific situations and to do our part and trust God and others to do theirs.

What is God's part to carry?

____

____

____

What is my part to carry?

____

____

____

Is there a part that someone else needs to carry?

____

____

____

This week, I will more keenly relax into the grace of God by worshiping through:

____

____

____

TOOL: RESTRAIN AND REFLECT

Social workers, chaplains, therapists, spiritual directors, and some pastors share a specific skill set that is unique to their vocation. They know how to restrain their initial impulses long enough to reflect on them and discern if they have what the situation requires. These people have learned to mistrust their unreliable narrator, or perhaps I should say, they have learned to hold back long enough to reflect on whether or not the narrator is *reliable.* They know they cannot automatically trust their initial impulses to say or do something. They realize they must pay attention to those impulses and manage them long enough to sift them through reality.

I find that my chronic anxiety and my unreliable narrator tend to block my awareness of God in the moment, but if I can restrain my impulses long enough to reflect on them with God, I have a much better chance of seeing reality. Sometimes after restraining and reflecting, I still do not know what to do, but I can relax into God's presence, knowing that God is with me and ahead of me.

A keen awareness of our recurring, predictable impulses can help us learn to control them. For example, I know that I am prone to show people I know an answer, to rush in and help when someone is just venting or sharing, and to agree to something to keep the peace or to please someone. That awareness can help me as I approach situations where I know my impulses will be triggered. I can ask God to help me restrain and to show me what God is actually calling me to do. The questions below can help us restrain and reflect.

These are my recurring impulses:

____

____

____

This is the next situation where I know my impulses will be activated:

____

____

____

Before that situation, I will stop and remember that God is with me and ahead of me by:

____

____

____

It typically takes ____________________ (fill in amount of time) for me to remember that God is with me.

THE NATURE OF EVERY GOSPEL

Before *gospel* was a church word, it was an empire word. In Jesus' time, the Roman Empire offered a gospel. They actually called it "good news." It was known as the Pax Romana ("Roman peace"), and it came from the "son of God"—Caesar Augustus. That gospel was brutal. It involved conquering towns and enslaving people, crucifying them, exploiting them, and squeezing them for all the taxes they could muster. If a person couldn't pay their tax to Rome, the empire would take their children as payment and use them as slaves. The "peace" of Rome was a carrot out of reach for most people. Only a few benefited. The majority paid.

There are many gospels besides the gospel of Jesus. If you simply think of a gospel as a "path to the good life" or a "path of good news," then you will see gospels everywhere. Almost every patriotic country has a gospel. The major world religions each have a different path to the good life. And our assumptions and reactivity are evidence that we're living for a gospel, trying to gain a good life.

Every gospel has three core elements: a promise, a path, and a payment.

I became a Christian when I was a teen. Before that, I was living for what I call the "gospel of 1980s Aussie teens." The promise was popularity, which promised fitting in and belonging. The path was to make a girl laugh, excel at academics, and be good at sports. (There was another teen gospel path—be weird—but I knew I was way too square to pull that off.) If you could carry out at least two out of the three steps, you would be fine. All three meant you were golden. All three meant you belonged with your peers, which was everything to me when I was a teen. All three meant that when I went home at the end of the day, I wouldn't have to replay everything in my mind and question how I would ever fit in. And that is where the payment comes in. As much as I walked the path to get the promise, I kept paying over and over again in my mind—profoundly insecure about facing friends and fitting in.

I was zero for three in that teen gospel and feeling lost and alone when Toni, my older sister, introduced me to the gospel of Jesus Christ. Toni had become a Christian a couple of years before. She was the only person in our extended family to become a follower of Jesus. I had felt lost as a teen, like I didn't fit in. It wasn't that no one liked me—I had friends at school and quite a good life—but I couldn't be myself, I couldn't relax. I always had to have a pretension or wear a mask to be loved. That is probably why I converted to Christianity. It was an incredible thing to be loved by the God of the universe, to be found by God.

In nearly every gospel, the human pays, and the god benefits. In Rome, the people paid, and Caesar and his cronies benefited. In the ancient Greek and Egyptian religions, the humans sacrificed crops or children, and the gods benefited. In the Aussie teen gospel, I paid and paid and paid. But I never could get the payoff; the promise I strived for was elusive.

Most gospels keep the promise always out of reach. We strive and strive but never reach it. Most gospels make us pay. If we want this life (promise), do these things (path and payment.)

The Stories We Tell Ourselves are gospels. So is The Way Things Are. Both offer a path and a promise, and both make us pay. My need to please people is a gospel. It puts me on a path with an offer of peace and freedom. My inner critic wants me to pay with condemnation and shame. But no matter how much I pay, I never get the payoff. Peace and freedom remain elusive.

TOOL: ANXIETY'S "GOSPEL"

Anxiety offers a "gospel" like any other gospel in that it offers a path to get a promise. And someone has to pay for someone else to benefit. As we have said, in every false gospel, the human pays for the sake of the god. So it is with anxiety. It makes us pay, mostly by making us do more of the same and pushing us to try harder. The other sign of a false gospel is we never get the payoff. Anxiety tells me I can worry my way to peace, but I never get that payoff; I only get more anxiety.

One of the most powerful anxiety management tools is to get clear on its "gospel."

What false paths have you followed in the past or are following now that you would like to explore?

____

____

____

____

What promises do those paths offer?

____

____

____

In those false paths, in what ways are you paying?

____

____

____

Are you getting the payoff?

____

____

____

It is amazing how many gospels we believe—how many paths we're on and how many promises we chase. We struggle to encounter God because we don't believe just one gospel; we believe many competing gospels, each putting us on a path, each keeping the promise out of reach, each making us pay.

Except one. In the gospel of Jesus, God pays for the sake of the human rather than the other way around. Jesus paid so we could get the promise.

One of the most powerful and liberating tools I use is paying attention to what I am believing at any given moment (my unreliable narrator) and then mapping out what the path is, what the promise is, and who is paying. If I am paying, then it is a false god. But in the one true gospel, *Jesus paid* so I can relax into the presence and sovereignty of God. This has nothing to do with being lazy or apathetic to the needs of this world. It has everything to do with being human-sized, worshiping God for being God-sized, and relaxing into the payment Jesus has already made on my behalf. I can follow this path and be free, and, most powerfully, I can actually experience the promise Jesus has for me—peace regardless of circumstances, love that I don't need to earn but is freely given, and freedom I feel in my body, not just believe in my head.

DISCUSSION QUESTIONS

1. What situation is coming up this week where you might practice "God with me, God ahead of me"?
2. As you look at the "God-Sized/Human-Sized" table, what impact on you and others did you list?
3. Do you have a situation coming up where you are carrying more than God has asked you to carry?
4. As you dig deeper into various gospels, what path have you been on?
5. Did you get the promise?
6. Who paid?
7. When have you been able to "relax into the presence of God"? What was that like for you?

SEVEN

GAP 3: MY SPIRITUAL PROGRESS

"I Thought I'd Be Further Along by Now"

Christian maturity is not a matter of doing more for God; it is God doing more in and through us.

EUGENE H. PETERSON, *PRACTICE RESURRECTION*

We have gone on a deep internal journey so far in this book. In the first chapter, I suggested that our faith is affected by four core dynamics: assumptions, reactivity, stuck patterns, and attempted solutions. We have been working through various internal ways these dynamics block our capacity to experience God's love and God's presence.

For this next gap, we turn our focus to our approach to Scripture. The reason we think we should be further along by now is connected to how we read the Bible, how we compare ourselves to others, and then how we reinforce these dynamics in our faith communities. I want to point out up front that it is quite possible that we *should* be further along in our faith. I am not suggesting that we get lazy and stop worrying about spiritual growth. I am proposing that our *attempted solutions* to this gap are the fundamental problem. The gap may be real, but our solutions are often fruitless. Many of us spend too much spiritual energy—and, frankly, guilt—trying to be something God did not ask us to be. We then spread that expectation around our faith communities and perpetuate the cycle. If we can notice the attempted solutions and therefore the stuck cycle we are in and get off that treadmill, we can open our souls to an encounter with God that can cause growth.

Let's start by looking at the way we relate to the Bible. We each bring many assumptions to our reading of Scripture. We project our assumptions onto the page and read those assumptions back from the page, thus reinforcing our stuck patterns. Assumptions are always easier to see in others than in ourselves, and when we're confronted by our own assumptions, it can be arresting or even threatening at first. When we look at the dynamics between Jesus and the Pharisees, much of their hostility was because Jesus was rummaging around in their assumptions, threatening what they thought they knew about Scripture.

BEING PETER

We could explore many assumptions related to our reading of Scripture, but I want to focus on those that relate to the spiritual progress we've made in our faith. Let's begin with a well-known story from the New Testament—Jesus' invitation to Peter to walk on water:

> Immediately Jesus made the disciples get into the boat and go on ahead of him to the other side, while he dismissed the crowd. After he had dismissed them, he went up on a mountainside by himself to pray. Later that night, he was there alone, and the boat was already a considerable distance from land, buffeted by the waves because the wind was against it.

> Shortly before dawn Jesus went out to them, walking on the lake. When the disciples saw him walking on the lake, they were terrified. "It's a ghost," they said, and cried out in fear.
>
> But Jesus immediately said to them: "Take courage! It is I. Don't be afraid."
>
> "Lord, if it's you," Peter replied, "tell me to come to you on the water."
>
> "Come," he said.
>
> Then Peter got down out of the boat, walked on the water and came toward Jesus. But when he saw the wind, he was afraid and, beginning to sink, cried out, "Lord, save me!"
>
> Immediately Jesus reached out his hand and caught him. "You of little faith," he said, "why did you doubt?"
>
> And when they climbed into the boat, the wind died down. Then those who were in the boat worshiped him, saying, "Truly you are the Son of God" (Matthew 14:22–33).

One helpful aspect of systems theory is the way it teaches us to notice the whole rather than the individual. On our own, we are prone to look at one person in a story and relate to that one person, but systems theory's gift is that it helps us gain a more holistic view. An individualistic approach to this passage might ask, "How can I step out in faith this week? What is Jesus beckoning me to do?" A systems approach says, "Wait just a hot minute! Eleven of the twelve disciples stayed in the boat. They still benefited from witnessing something astonishing, and they all ended up worshiping Jesus." In this story, most of Jesus' disciples—92 percent to be precise—did not step out in faith at all. In fact, they sat in the boat and watched as their impetuous and bold friend stepped out. Is the only right interpretation of this story that Peter was the good disciple and all the others were bad? Maybe rather than trying to be like Peter this week, we should try to be like one of the other eleven. This week, less Peter, more Thaddeus. Perhaps we could start a campaign: #TeamThaddeus.

ASSUMPTION 1: We must always be like the main character of any Bible story.

REALITY: We will grow in Christ sooner once we accept that we are very much like ourselves, and none of us can—or should—always be like the main character of any given Bible story.

If you are prone toward action like Peter was, then go for it. You may well be a personality type that is energized by risk. You may also be prone to act first and think later. But what if you are the kind of person who, when invited to do something new or risky, first creates a spreadsheet to assess all options, along with a cost-benefit analysis? By the time you're done listing all the risk liabilities, a soaking-wet Peter and a laughing Jesus are back in the boat with you. Is that bad? Can you love spreadsheets and risk mitigation plans and still walk by faith?

Or must we all be like Peter all the time? What is it about us humans that draws us toward carrying the pressure and guilt of thinking we really should be someone else?

This leads to a second vital point. If we look carefully at this text, it ends with all twelve of the disciples worshiping Jesus in astonishment. Maybe the text is more about being astonished at Jesus than it is about us taking a faith risk. Maybe the central point of this story is Jesus' power, not Peter's faith steps. Those of us in cultures that place a high value on performance and improvement are prone to see every story in the Bible as "something I need to work on," but much of Scripture is actually designed to help us worship our astonishing God. In other words, maybe Peter isn't the main character of this story; maybe it's Jesus.

What if most of the stories in the Bible are designed to *primarily* evoke a worship encounter with God rather than a self-improvement task list? We would do well, particularly those of us in production-based cultures, to be suspicious of our relentless need to improve and grow. If we're reading the text with our minds always thinking we have something to work on, we may be missing the heart of God. Maybe God is less concerned with our improvement and more concerned with our worship.

The text clearly shows we can stay in the boat, watch our friend almost drown, and still end up worshiping Jesus. Now *there* is a sermon waiting to be preached! "Friends, this week, I don't recommend stepping out in faith. I recommend staying in the boat and watching your friend take steps. You'll end up worshiping Jesus either way!"

While we're on the topic of walking by faith, we ought to pause to reflect on whether that is what Peter was actually doing. If you revisit the text, Jesus never *invited* Peter to step out in faith; Peter *asked* if he could walk toward Jesus. If Peter had never asked, would Jesus have even invited him? Did Jesus particularly care whether or not Peter could walk on water? Probably not, if the primary point of this story is Jesus' sovereignty over the elements. We take this story as an example of walking by faith when it could just as easily be a story about Jesus thinking to himself, *Well, there goes Peter again. Let's see how this ends up.*

By this time, of course, my social media campaign of #TeamThaddeus is probably gaining some traction. Who is Thaddeus, by the way? What do we know about him? Very little. We actually know very little about most of the faithful followers in the Bible, which is one reason we put so much pressure on ourselves to become like the ones we do know. We are all wrestling to follow Jesus well, and it can feel like such an intangible experience that we want to find some tangible way to do it.

ASSUMPTION 2: We see ourselves as the center of most stories. We start from a place of self as the primary agent in a story.

REALITY: God designed Scripture to primarily engage *God* first and foremost in worship and astonishment. All change is derived from encountering God, not trying hard to be like another person.

ASSUMPTION 3: We know little about most of God's followers in the Bible, and we are anxious to follow Jesus well, so we focus exclusively on the followers we do know something about.

REALITY: Steve's #TeamThaddeus campaign is probably viral already. Join the revolution! Okay, just kidding.

ACTUAL REALITY: God invites us into a journey of becoming our true self, not someone else.

How many times have you read or heard about Peter walking on water? For me, the number has to be more than fifty times, maybe even one hundred times. And each time, my first impulse is to wonder if I am walking by faith *enough* or how I can step out in faith in the days ahead. I begin with me as the center point. My first impulse is not to pause and be astonished at the miraculous God who is worthy of my worship. But when I intentionally orient around God as the center point, I still consider walking by faith—but only *after* I have first set my eyes on Jesus as the center of it all.

WONDERFULLY LIMITED HUMAN BEINGS

I may have thought about this passage fifty-plus times, but I often forget that Peter only walked on water once. That seems a bit unfair. Peter walked on water one time, but because I read that story over and over and because I live with low-grade anxiety and guilt about not being a good enough follower, I feel the need to *be stepping out in faith* for my whole lifetime. Remember, Peter asked to step out; Jesus did not invite him to do so. How does that change the story for us?

ASSUMPTION 4: We read these Bible stories multiple times and forget that many of these experiences happened only once to a particular person. We carry the pressure to live out that one story in our lives all the time.

REALITY: Seeing these stories as points in time rather than for all time can help us relax into human-sized expectations.

We are all quite different from each other, aren't we? Let's look at another well-known story that features very different personalities from Peter—Mary and Martha and their response to Jesus in their home. Luke is our guide for this story (see Luke 10). Jesus and his disciples stop by Martha and Mary's house for dinner while they are passing through the village. Let's face it, preparing a meal for at least fifteen people is quite an undertaking, especially if they didn't get much advance notice.

Martha is understandably stressed over the final preparations. Martha's sister, Mary, isn't lifting a finger to help, so Martha rats on her sister to Jesus: "Lord, don't you care that my sister has left me to do the work by myself? Tell her to help me!" (Luke 10:40). Jesus then chides Martha for being "worried and upset about many things, but few things are needed—or indeed only one. Mary has chosen what is better, and it will not be taken away from her" (verses 41–42).

First of all, can we all agree that Mary is probably Martha's *younger* sister. Also, I need to confess that I am Team Martha. Someone has to do the dishes so people can eat! I am more prone toward activity than contemplation. But still, our tendency when we read this story is to feel guilt over our own hurried pace and busyness, not focused on what matters most. We see ourselves like Martha—"worried and upset about many things"—and we think we need to be more like Mary, who chose the "better" thing, abiding with Jesus and his teachings while the meal got cold.

ASSUMPTION 5: One week we need to be like Peter. The next week we need to be like Mary. It all depends on what story we are reading that week.

REALITY: Peter was pretty much always like Peter. Mary was very Maryesque. You are you, and I am me. We will get further in our faith if we accept our humanity than if we always strive to be someone or something we can never be.

Peter walked on water once, but his propensity was to live with courage and boldness throughout his following of Jesus. Before Jesus' resurrection, Peter got it wrong more often than he got it right. He was bold, yes, but often boldly wrong. I can relate to that. I, like Peter, have a bold personality, and I am prone to action first and thinking later. After the resurrection, Peter seemed to get it right more often than wrong. This is the heart of following Jesus. We are generally like ourselves, but Jesus' transformation doesn't completely alter our personality to make us a well-rounded human. Instead, Jesus helps us become our best self.

Some of us are bold and take risks. Some of us love books more than people and are quietly thoughtful. Some of us know how to create a safe space for people to open up. Some of us inspire people to take action and fight for social justice.

But none of us are much like the other. There is room in you to be exactly one human, and God wants to transform you—not into a superdisciple, but into a human-sized you. God made you and invites you to let God redeem, heal, and deploy your wiring and personality, just as you are.

Now we start to see other dynamics at play. The pressure to be like Peter one week, Mary the next, and so on generates significant reactivity in us that, as we discovered in previous chapters, causes us to stop noticing God. Rather than relaxing into being human-sized, we move into a stuck pattern of *trying to be like all of the characters we read about*. We often do this under our own steam. Our posture is not naturally to first encounter God and invite God to be the change agent. Our first move is to anxiously work on ourselves or feel guilt over not being further along or better at becoming a superdisciple. Our attempted solutions become the shoulds and oughts of our lives, and we spin around and around in that cycle.

SUPERDISCIPLES

We could have chosen dozens of stories for our second example because we are prone to focus on the application of each particular text in front of us. We could have looked to Ruth's faithfulness or Esther's courage or Paul's stunning intellect or Joseph's moral compass or even Jael's tent-peg skills. There are hundreds of people in the Bible, and we tend to take the details of each story as something for us to strive toward. Over time, we end up stacking all of these people with all of their unique traits and examples into one fictional superdisciple that none of us will ever be and, frankly, none of them were either.

The people in the Bible were just living their one life, trying to keep up with God or figure out how to follow Jesus. In our readings of the text, we can strip them of their complexity and keep them in the two-dimensional realm. We can treat them more as examples than as human beings. We take them as a collective whole, creating an impossible standard for ourselves that they themselves never had to achieve.

Imagine being told you should be more like a supermodel. You look in the mirror, and you know there is no way you can do it. You simply do not have the bone structure. You will never be a supermodel. I have had to grapple with this grave realization lately. Now that I am getting older, my wife has encouraged me to take care of my skin, so I recently started a facial regimen twice per day that involves a cleanser, hyaluronic acid, and a moisturizer. Occasionally I even add an under-eye bag cream. This is new territory for me. I have never in my life taken care of my skin, but I have to confess that this new regimen feels and looks amazing. You should see me now. But even with my new dewy and milky features, there is no risk that I'll be mistaken for a supermodel. Trying harder won't get me there. I simply don't have the frame and features for it. I will always just be me.

Imagine being told to be more like Albert Einstein or Mother Teresa or Winston Churchill. Now imagine being encouraged to imitate all three at once. Each of these people is a stunning historical figure who changed our world, but none of them are much like the other, and none of us are anything like them. It is worth noting that many of the people in the Bible are in the same category. They are once-in-history kinds of people. God used these people to create once-in-history situations. As long as we compare our one self with their collective selves, and as long as we expect ourselves to always be some version of all of them for all time, we will stay stuck in this gap.

I don't believe God limited his unique work to Bible times. God is always doing unique work in the world and always using stunning and remarkable people. But some of us, maybe even most of us, are more like Martha than Mary, more like Thaddeus than Peter, and more like the church members Paul wrote to than Paul himself. We are more like the unnamed people in the New Testament who participated in faith communities, worked to put food on the table, and lived quiet lives. Our world today absolutely has remarkable people whose impact for God is immense. I am inspired by these folks and genuinely thank God for them. I try to be a person who impacts people for God's kingdom too. I am not in any way speaking against them, but if you are not one of those people, I want you to know that being 100 percent human-sized is all God ever asked you to be.

What I am writing about is quite nuanced because many of us have been deeply comforted or challenged by these very texts I am sharing. The problem isn't any one story. I chose the stories of Peter walking on water and Mary sitting with Jesus because they offer a stark contrast, but the fact is, God has used these stories to profoundly shape my faith. As I look back on my decades of following Jesus, some of the most indelible moments have been when I sensed God calling me to step into my fear, trust God, and walk into something I couldn't fully see or fully make sense of. Frankly, writing this book has been a faith-stretching experience. I also feel rightly convicted that, like Martha, I am prone to get wrapped up in the hustle and the tasks. I need reminding that God is right there with me, and I can relax into God's presence anytime. The tasks can wait; the hurry will never go away.

Maybe it is the same for you. Maybe much of your faith life has been shaped by these stories. This is a nuanced situation, isn't it? For me, the problem is not the stories, and it is certainly not the Bible. It is my approach, my stuck patterns, and my attempted solutions. This is why, at the very beginning of this book, I mentioned that I needed to step away from the "faithy things" to notice some patterns so that when I stepped back into the faithy things, I was able to engage them in a healthier and more fruitful way.

The irony is, we probably *should* do better, know better, and be better, but staying on this exhausting treadmill of comparison, trying harder, and doing more of the same is not the way to get there.

MIRACLES PER PAGE AND MUNDANE DAYS

Have you ever struggled with the gap between the seeming miraculous life of the early disciples compared to your rather mundane life? The authors of Scripture have little interest in the mundane moments of life. They offer a truncated history, focusing on the God-soaked moments. We never see the disciples shopping for groceries or doing laundry, or, frankly, engaging in recreation. And so we embrace the impression that they were always doing faithy things, but, in reality, they must have had relaxing nights and mundane days. Jesus' public ministry lasted between 1,200 and 1,250 days, about three to three and a half years. How many of those public ministry days do you think the gospel authors recorded?

When I researched this, I was shocked to discover that John records twenty unique days of Jesus' ministry in his gospel. Out of Jesus' 1,200-plus days, John recorded about twenty of them. No wonder John wrote at the end of his gospel, "Jesus did many other things as well. If every one of them were written down, I suppose that even the whole world would not have room for the books that would be written" (21:25). If you count every unique day captured by all the gospel writers, the total number is between fifty-two and fifty-seven. The Gospels capture less than 5 percent of Jesus' public ministry. What did he and the disciples do with the other 95 percent of their time?

ASSUMPTION 6: Every day for Jesus' first followers was God-soaked. Something is wrong with me, or I am doing something wrong because I don't have many God-soaked days.

REALITY: Scripture authors recorded a truncated history to show us who God is. Jesus and the first followers experienced many mundane days.

When we read the Gospels, miracles seem to be flying around all over the place. We see Jesus like Oprah, dishing out miracles left and right. "You get a miracle, and you get a miracle! Everybody gets a miracle!" But the reality was quite different. The gospel writers record thirty-seven total miracles of Jesus. If we count the total miracles recorded in all of Scripture, that number is 125. That is 125 miracles in approximately eighteen hundred years of recorded history. Of course, Jesus performed miracles that were not recorded, yet our illusion that every day was a miracle-soaked day is far from reality.

The primary reason for Jesus' miracles was to point to God's kingdom and character. Jesus, of course, had great compassion on people as he healed them, but even when Jesus healed individuals, he usually did it for a greater goal of showing God's kingdom. Frankly, sometimes it seems as though Jesus healed people just so he could annoy the Pharisees. You could go back through the Gospels and count how many miracles Jesus performed out of what looks like spite!

As a pastor, I have had countless people beg me to beg God for a miracle. I understand the desperation, as I have begged God for plenty of miracles myself. I have had precious friends die too young, and I have had friends whose children have succumbed to awful diseases. A lot of my prayers over the decades have sounded something like, "God, you can do this. Please heal." When we see so many people being healed in the Bible and when we know God is able, it can be difficult to reconcile a lack of healing in our own spheres. It can make us wonder if it all is true and if God is truly good and capable. My faith is helped when I see the reality of the healing ratios in Scripture.

ASSUMPTION 7: God did a lot more miracles in the Bible than take place today, and they were always for the individual's benefit.

REALITY: Miracles per page in the Bible may seem high, but those miracles spread out over history is a low number. Jesus did many miracles for reasons beyond the benefit to the individual.

I get particularly itchy when I open my Bible to Acts 2. Many of us church leaders love us some Acts 2! Here is the favorite part of your average church leader:

> They devoted themselves to the apostles' teaching and to fellowship, to the breaking of bread and to prayer. Everyone was filled with awe at the many wonders and signs performed by the apostles. All the believers were together and had everything in common. They sold property and possessions to give to anyone who had need. Every day they continued to meet together in the temple courts. They broke bread in their homes and ate together with glad and sincere hearts, praising God and enjoying the favor of all the people. And the Lord added to their number daily those who were being saved. (Acts 2:42–47)

We love the purity of this season in the life of the early church. Nowadays, community is so messy and complex, isn't it? But we open our Bible to Acts 2 and see the church in its purest, most ideal form. A multitude of churches hold Acts 2 as the gold standard of church. It is such a beautiful, pure, and compelling vision.

Do you know a church that was not striving to become an Acts 2 church? The church in Acts 2. They weren't striving for the outcome. They didn't create a vision statement. They were simply responding to their miraculous encounter with the Holy Spirit. We read how the early believers sold possessions and gave radically, and we feel we should do the same. Maybe we should. But if I were in church and the woman giving the announcements suddenly had a ball of fire rest on her head and began speaking fluently in Farsi because several Iranian refugees were in attendance, and then if she mentioned that those refugees needed a car, I would probably donate my car too. Too often we expect the radical outcome without the radical impetus. Yes, we ought to be radically generous, but also, yes, the radical generosity of the early believers was fueled by a radical encounter with God's physical and tangible presence.

The early church in Acts 2 lived in a harsh empire with short life spans and an intense presence of the Holy Spirit. Many of us live in far different cultural conditions with a far less tangible presence of God. I don't intend for us to be lazy, but as long as we expect the radical result without the miraculous work of God first, we will stay on the more-of-the-same and try-harder treadmills, and we will not grow. It simply does not work to read about the early church in Acts and then try harder to be more like them. This only leads to legalistic bondage, not an encounter with the risen Christ.

Here is another truth about the Acts 2 church: it didn't stay the Acts 2 church for long. I love Paul's letters to the churches in the New Testament because so many of them have a grumpy tone. Paul had to scold the people in Corinth because some of them were sleeping with their stepmothers and others were elbowing their way to the front of the Communion line. He came out swinging against the church in Galatia for its syncretistic practices and because it was polluting the gospel of grace with legalism. Paul was compelled to write to the people in Rome because some of them thought the best way to activate more grace was to sin more. Paul even had to confront Peter over his ethnic preferences and his tendency toward favoritism. He had to strong-arm a wealthy property owner to embrace his former slave as a brother and to forgive him. So many of the New Testament letters contain correction from Paul to people who had been living for Jesus for a while. They were long past the purity of Acts 2.

Acts 2 is beautiful, breathtaking, inspiring, and the absolute pure work of God's Spirit. It is also short-term. The letters to Corinth, Rome, and Galatia show the more long-term, realistic view of church community.

As a pastor, I confess to occasionally lamenting the spiritual state of some congregants. I've left a handful of pastoral counseling encounters after someone has shared with me their life choices and the consequences they are facing, and I found myself questioning whether I am effectively helping people grow in their faith.

Then I read 1 Corinthians, and I feel *much* better about myself!

(To my own congregants: If you're reading this, it is most certainly not you. It was probably the guy sitting next to you in church. Don't worry about it!)

ASSUMPTION 8: If we just try harder, we will be more like the church in Acts 2.

REALITY: As long as we're better than the Corinthians, we'll be okay.

ACTUAL REALITY: The pure response of Acts 2 happens when we encounter God in tangible and supernatural ways. Miraculous speaking of foreign languages and mysterious balls of fire on our heads will produce a pure revival response; more rallying of effort will not. Humans make things messy over time.

THE FINAL COMPARISON FRONTIER

One pattern that has concerned me for years is our use of "be like Jesus" or "become like Jesus" language. It concerns me because I think our tendency is to fall into the same more-of-the-same and try-harder patterns that fail us when we try to act like characters in the Bible. You might rightly say, "Jesus isn't like any other people in the Bible." I couldn't agree more.

Jesus is not like anyone in the Bible, and Jesus is not like any of us. Jesus is fully God and fully human. We are fully human, and we will never be a god, let alone fully God. Some religious cults teach that we can become gods one day, but Christianity teaches that the entire problem of us humans is the way we try to be our own god or worship any number of false gods. God's job is to form us into Christlikeness, but we are prone to make it our job because we so quickly move into the seat of control. As we dig deeper into the New Testament's teachings and Jesus' own teaching, we may be startled to discover that the primary emphasis of our own spiritual growth effort is not so much becoming like another person or like God; it is dying to self.

We cannot be like Jesus, because when we try, we end up creating Jesus in our image and losing sight of the true Jesus. Some of us really appreciate the side of Jesus that is gentle and kind. We like the Jesus who beckons the little children to come to him and who gently restores Peter after he denied Christ. Others of us are strongly driven by justice and love the prophetic and confrontational side of Jesus. We like the Jesus who turns over tables in the temple, makes a whip out of cords, and stands up to the Pharisees, calling them "blind guides" (Matthew 15:14). In our effort to be more like our favorite aspect of Jesus, we lose sight of who Jesus truly is and instead we make Christ in our own image. Jesus becomes an idealized version of ourselves.

When we use "be like Christ" or "Christlike" language, I think we often mean "become a better person who reflects Christ's values, character, and behavior." That is a worthy and good goal. Paul makes a list of such character traits when he writes that the fruit of the Spirit is "love, joy, peace, patience, kindness, goodness, faithfulness, gentleness, and self-control" (Galatians 5:22–23 NLT). When we think of being like Jesus, we're mostly thinking about this list. But our tendency is to read the fruit of the Spirit, do a self-evaluation, and decide that we're falling short. Maybe we see that we're not very patient, so we commit to work on being more patient. Maybe we do some activities and habits that force us to become more patient. At the end of the week, we see that the work has paid off. We actually are a more patient person now. Congratulations, after a week's effort, you have become a more patient legalist. You have participated in the fruit of the human, not the fruit of the Spirit.

The fruit of the Spirit is what God forms in us *after we die to* ourselves. Paul talks about how "Christ is formed in you" in Galatians 4:19, and I think he uses the passive voice for a reason. It is something Christ does to us on the other side of us dying to ourselves. If you want to become a more patient person, the more fruitful endeavor is to notice what makes you impatient, and die to that. Having died, God is good to God's word. God's resurrection and life-renewing power will form you. Will you become a more patient person? Possibly, but it is ultimately God's job to form us, not ours. Our job is to keep dying to self, allowing God to reveal areas where we are depending on self rather than depending on God.

The issue with "being like Jesus" language is how quickly we confuse the division of labor. Humans are simply so used to being in control that we assume the formation seat, and we unintentionally work on our own formation rather than die to self so God can form us. Our job is to die to self. God's job is to form us into his image.

Time-tested spiritual practices and endeavors like prayer and reading our Bibles are not primarily designed to make us better people. They are designed to help us encounter Christ. Many of us live in cultures that highly value improvement and progress, so we do not realize that we transfer that pressure onto God. Of course, there is nothing intrinsically wrong with working on our patience or self-control; it might be a very good and needed endeavor. But remember that humans are prone to falling into stuck patterns, and one of the hardest to dislodge is our tendency to drive our own life. God is more interested in us bringing our whole selves to him in worship than he is in our improvement.

I find it helpful to get off the treadmill of trying to be like Christ and instead focus my effort on dying to self, especially my reactivity and assumptions. Then I focus on who Christ is and what Christ has done and is doing. That focus is what causes me to worship and encounter Christ. God takes care of the rest.

I must also confess that after dying to self over and again for a couple of decades now, the stark reality is, I am still pretty much like me. I carry the same triggers, beliefs, reactivity, and false needs. God's formation has definitely changed me, but it hasn't changed me into a different person. God has changed me to seek him sooner when I am reactive rather than addressing my shortcomings on my own like I used to.

The fundamental issue is about the division of labor, the source of power, and, ultimately, worship. I am highly suspicious of my need to always be the driver, always at the wheel, working on improvement. "Must do better! Must be better" is futile. But coming to Christ, offering my body as a living sacrifice as Paul teaches in Romans 12, and letting God renew my mind into his will? I can do that again and again and again. This practice, which is hard and takes time, produces worship in me.

There is room in the body of Christ for all types of human-sized followers. According to Paul in 1 Corinthians 12, some of us are elbows, and some are eyes, and some are knees, and some are the smallest toes, but all are equally essential to the kingdom of God. Jesus is the head. We will never be the head. Jesus is the life force and the King. We get to do our part in the way God has made and called us.

One follower of Jesus can take bold risks, one can sit quietly and soak, one can faithfully balance spreadsheets, while another challenges us to stretch. One would much rather repair cars for people in need than pray in public or talk about Scripture; another likes to be financially generous but struggles to serve in any public way. One follower can hold a steady job, live a life of dignity, be faithful in their relationships, and live a quiet life, while another can launch a powerful organization that stops human trafficking. Of course, there are all manner of people in between these examples.

If we focus primarily on dying to ourselves and worshiping Jesus—seeking to encounter the true Christ—we can ease into being human-sized, relax into God's presence, and be free to serve, sacrifice, and be stretched, challenged, and rebuked. We are free to repent because we no longer need pretense. We are free to make mistakes and follow God's Spirit. God deploys us as imperfect humans—animated, energized, and renewed by God's Spirit—into this broken and troubled world.

DISCUSSION QUESTIONS

1. Are you prone to try to always be like the main character of every Bible story? What has that been like for you?
2. Is there a person in Scripture you most relate to? What attributes do you share?
3. How can God redeem and use those attributes for the sake of others?
4. How would you say a person grows in Christ?
5. How do you discern God's will today?
6. What aspects of following Jesus were more straightforward in Bible times, and what aspects were more difficult?
7. What most helps you encounter the invisible God today?

EIGHT

REPLACING UNHEALTHY ASSUMPTIONS

Goodness and beauty can prevail in the face of overwhelming shame.
CURT THOMPSON, *THE SOUL OF SHAME*

We took quite a journey in that last chapter, so let's begin with a couple of tools to help us integrate those ideas and replace unhealthy assumptions about our spiritual progress with something better. Can it really be true that we can faithfully follow Jesus, grow in our faith, and serve in God's mission by becoming more like ourselves and not worrying so much about becoming like other people—even Jesus?

Begin by making a list of things Jesus can do that you and your friends will never be able to do, no matter how hard you try:

-
-
-
-

That list is the reason Jesus is worthy of our worship. Jesus knows what it is like to be human, so he can relate to us, but at the same time because he is fully God, he is utterly distinct and worthy of our worship. Pause now to thank God for what he can do that you will never be able to do.

If your side of the division of labor is dying to self, what area of your life do you struggle to release to God? Is there a relationship or a habit or an irritability? The way I die to self is to give those things to God. List them below:

-
-
-
-
-

In my experience, dying to self is not a one-and-done thing but an ongoing practice, which means we have to be patient with ourselves. If you have listed many things above, you might prioritize by circling the one that feels smallest to you and the one that feels most overwhelming. If you find yourself easily irritable with someone, that might be small. If you carry a significant secret addiction, that one is big.

Note: If you are harboring something big, you cannot die to it privately. It must be done in community. I highly encourage you to find a group that specializes in helping with those big areas of destructive secret habits. Some destructive secret habits might be addictions, in which case one of the twelve-step groups might be your next step. If you find yourself in the grip of something large that's eating you up, like severe depression, please take the brave step of asking for help.

Because my default is toward self-improvement rather than worship, I find it helpful to schedule times of intentional worship so I can relax into God's presence.

Can you find certain times on your calendar when you will intentionally step into worshiping God in this next month?

-
-
-
-
-

TOOL: THE LIFE-GIVING LIST

Okay, so you've set time on your calendar for worship. What do you actually *do* during that time? Some people talk about spending time with God like it is the most natural thing in the world, but maybe you're not sure what to do during that time. Maybe if you're being honest, you try to read your Bible but not much happens, or you find your mind wandering when you pray. If so, you're normal. And there are things you can do to help.

For the last several years, I have hosted a podcast where I interview guests. After asking them about their expertise, I turn the tables and ask them about my field—chronic anxiety—and how it impacts their well-being. I ask them a set of questions I playfully call the "gauntlet of anxiety questions." The final question is my favorite: "When in your life recently have you felt most fully and completely loved?"

As of the writing of this book, I have interviewed 124 guests. The most common response is a pause and a deep exhale. I like that. We are all on the hunt for home—that experience of being fully and completely loved, relaxing into God's presence.

That is the question that helped me create what I call the Life-Giving List. The Life-Giving List is simply a list of the people, places, and activities God has given you that make you feel human, connected, and alive. The list includes activities that take a few minutes as well as those that take several days. It includes places in and around your home as well as places that require travel. It is an extensive and intentional list that captures God's goodness to you. I have included a blank Life-Giving List in an appendix at the back of the book, or you can visit www.stevecusswords.com/resources to download a digital one.

The list helps me stub my toe on God's love and presence in small and grand ways, and I use the list in my daily connection with God. I also use my calendar and budget to make time for the longer and larger items on the list.

The Life-Giving List has six columns. The first column is "People," and the second column is "Remote or Local?" Make a list of the people God has put in your life who are life-giving. Are they in town or out of town? That information will become helpful shortly. Column three is "Places," and column four is "Distance from My House." Column five is "Activities," and column six is "Cost of Money and Time."

Here is how I use it. The People column is pretty straightforward. Who are the people whom God has put in your life who help you feel at home? Put those people on your list. For Places, I encourage you to start right inside your home. It can be as simple as the chair where you read Scripture or a garden in your yard. Begin with places in your home and proceed out from there. On my Life-Giving List, some of the places include a brown leather chair in my home, our kitchen counter, the prayer labyrinth at our church, a monastery one hour from my home, some specific beaches, and Assisi, Italy. I have many other places too, but hopefully these examples will help you start your list. I encourage you to be as specific and concrete as possible in capturing local and remote places.

For Activities, try to list at least twenty or thirty activities that take just a few minutes and that don't cost money. Then add activities that might take more budgeting of money and time. Some activities on my list include holding my wife's hand, playing acoustic guitar, the first time I see or hear from my kids in a day, rubbing my dog's floppy ears, watching stand-up comedy, reading my Bible, looking at the mountains near where I live, listening to a vinyl album, and praying for people. These activities take a few minutes. Here are some longer activities for me: a day of fishing in a trout stream with a life-giving friend; a road trip with my family; a long, slow dinner with life-giving people; hiking with my wife; and chanting Gregorian chants with the Benedictine nuns at the monastery up the road.

I have more than 160 items on my Life-Giving List. Some are mundane (like scratching my dog's floppy ears), and some are grand (like sipping cappuccinos in Assisi). I have things on my list that I have done one time in my life and may never do again—like going to Assisi.

I use the list as a worship document. It started out as a deeply personal and particular need. As a pastor, I had cultivated the bad habit of giving away God's gifts but not receiving them for myself. I was prone to focus on others, help others, and share my gifts with them. Of course, these are very good things to do, but I was out of balance. I've shared previously in this book my tendency to not receive God's love for myself, and during my 2016 epiphany, God convicted me that I needed to learn to receive God's gifts for me. God has given me some gifts to share with others, but actually many of the gifts of God were just for me as God's beloved child.

What has God given to you that reminds you that you are God's child? What gifts make you feel human and alive? To get specific and concrete, start working on your Life-Giving List.

When I do these activities and find myself in these places and spend time with these people, I pause and thank God that God is so good. Each time I participate in a life-giving habit, I intentionally connect with God in gratitude. We got our dog as a puppy during the COVID isolation of 2020, and he has been such a gift to our family through some difficult times. He is now very addicted to ear rubs and boldly approaches me for one several times a day. When I rub his ears, which takes thirty seconds to a minute, I pray a prayer of thanks to God for generously providing this dog. I also remember that God made me a human, which means God imbued me with the capacity for joy, love, laughter, and beauty. Likewise, when I listen to a piece of music and am moved by the beauty or wonder of it, I thank God.

This simple Life-Giving List tool helps me relax into God's presence several times a day. When we are wrapped up in ourselves, when we are self-righteous, we forget the Lord. We get solemn and weighed down. The Life-Giving List helps me bump up against the love and goodness of God every day. I use the list proactively by cultivating twelve to fifteen life-giving habits per day and by calendaring life-giving habits and people that take more planning. I also use the list reactively. If I find myself falling into anxiety, earnestness, or any form of self-righteousness, I pull out my list and do some things on it.

Most of us intuitively know the people, places, and activities that make us feel human and alive, but we don't take that extra step of thanking God for them or using them as a trigger to notice God and relax into God's presence. The Life-Giving List helps me increase my threshold for worship, and, perhaps most powerfully, it massively expands my scope and palette of what worship is. Of course, the items on the list are not all equal. I believe Scripture is authoritative in my life, and my dog's ears are not. Prayer connects me to the heart of God, while stand-up comedy provides a few minutes of relief. The point is to massively expand our awareness of God's goodness to us so we can lower our threshold to worship each day.

The most valuable part of the Life-Giving List is how it increases the scope of God's gifts to us and our awareness of them. How about starting on your list today? Go on an intentional hunt for the love of God this month, and see if you can add thirty items to your list. Then you can cultivate a rhythm of life-giving encounters to run into God's presence and goodness.

TOOL: BIBLE STUDY, PRAYER, AND QUIET TIME

You may be wondering about the more typical spiritual practices and where they fit in. These items are on my Life-Giving List, although they are often listed more concretely. I don't just list "prayer"; I list several different types of prayer: "pray for a friend"; "pray for a conflict somewhere in the world"; "give thanks"; "ask God for a word for the day"; "remember what is true"; "spend a few minutes in silence with God"; "read a prayer from history"; "read the Lord's Prayer"; and so on. For Bible study, I list things like, "read a chapter from the Old Testament and the New Testament"; "read one verse and reflect on it through the day"; "listen to a Bible app"; and so on. Of course I do not do all these things every day—actually, I do not do any of them every day—but most days, I am in God's Word and saying prayers.

The problem with these more typical disciplines is twofold. First, we have narrowed the way to engage them, so rather than *enjoy* the Bible, we have limited ourselves to a Bible reading plan or a formula that we need to perform correctly. To clarify, if a Bible reading plan works for you, that is fantastic, but some people will gain more if they widen their palette for engaging in it. The same is true for prayer. Sometimes prayer doesn't do much for us because we use only one way of praying rather than many different ways. There are so many ways to engage God in Scripture and prayer. Maybe try adding a few different colors to your palette you haven't yet tried.

The second issue is that, as a pastor, I have a competitive advantage over some of you in my Bible study. I went to Bible college and graduated with a major in Bible and a minor in preaching. I also have a Master of Divinity degree, which is a particularly heavy master's degree that includes a hefty Bible and theology section. I'll be frank. Before college and graduate school, I was biblically illiterate. I couldn't put Abraham, Isaac, and Jacob in the correct birth order. My college and graduate school experiences were absolutely exhilarating in the way they helped me navigate and engage Scripture. Also, for years I was paid to spend significant time each week studying Scripture to craft sermons. All that to say, please do not be discouraged if you lack Bible knowledge or if you struggle to engage your Bible. I struggled too before I received so much training.

Feeling guilty about our deficiencies, comparing ourselves to others, or giving up on engaging in Bible study and prayer isn't the solution. Thanks to the internet, we have free access to world-class scholars and tools that were previously only available if we went to college or graduate school. Equipping you with tools and resources to help in your Bible study and prayer is beyond the scope of this book. If I were starting this journey, I would ask a local Bible nerd I trust to recommend a book or an online resource. I suggest that, rather than opening your Bible and beginning to read, you focus on one Bible book and consult resources along with it. For example, if I were reading Genesis, I would buy a book by a scholar that helps me understand Genesis, and I would engage the BibleProject on YouTube and watch their videos on Genesis.

TOOL: GET CLEAR ON WHO YOU ARE IN CHRIST

As we look at the characters in the Bible, we see that they have tendencies and traits in the same way we have tendencies and traits. In particular, two of these characters are helpful to us because we are able to get a clear picture of *who they were before* they experienced a profound encounter with Jesus and *who they were after*—Peter and Paul. While they generally had the same traits before and after being transformed by Jesus, we see that God redeemed those traits from tendencies that were destructive and full of self to tendencies that were utilized in God's service. As they followed Jesus, they became more like themselves. The vision for this sort of spiritual growth is to accept that we are made by God the way we are. We no longer need to pour effort into being something or someone we are not. If we can accept who we are, we are free to invite God to redeem and transform our personality, wiring, and proclivities for God's purpose.

Look at this table with examples, and consider some of your own traits. You may need your friends or a group you are part of to help you see what traits you have that are unique to you—traits that God can use for God's kingdom and for service to others. What do your friends and community say is your unique contribution to God's kingdom? What are you good at when you are at your best, and in what ways are you a blessing to the world? I have included a couple of my own traits as an example.

PERSON	BEFORE AN ENCOUNTER WITH CHRIST	AFTER AN ENCOUNTER WITH CHRIST
Peter	Bold, impetuous, put his foot in his mouth, prone to act without thinking first.	Bold, courageous, took charge in Acts 2 to proclaim the gospel, refused to be silenced by threats.
Paul	Brilliant, had to be right, zealous to the point of violence, focused mostly on Jewish people.	Brilliant, persuaded people to become Christ-followers based on his intellect, focused on all people.
Steve	Engaging with people, needs to make them laugh or happy, needs to be needed.	Engaging with people, able to create true community in a group, advocates for people in need and equips them.
Me		

CULTURAL FORMATION, FLIPPED VALUES, AND PAUL

If you've traveled out of your own culture, you have discovered how profoundly humans are shaped by their cultural context. My first ever cross-cultural experience was when I was a foreign exchange student in Japan in high school. I grew up in Perth, Western Australia, which is directly south of Japan. In the 1980s, it was cheaper for Japanese people to fly to Perth and play golf than to play golf in Japan, so Japanese became a helpful language to learn. When I graduated, I was 60 to 70 percent fluent and could read two of the three written Japanese alphabets, along with about five hundred characters of the third alphabet, Kanji. I can still speak a little bit of Japanese. *Boku wa, sukoshi nihongo o hanashimashta.* Feel free to use Google Translate so you can marvel at my Japanese language skills.

My student exchange experience in Japan was my first-ever plunge into a different culture. I lived there for a month with a Japanese family. Of course, the food was different and fantastic, but the values, religion, and way of life were very different too. The first night, after having taken a traditional Japanese bath, I had to go straight to bed afterward. It simply sapped all energy from my body. I haven't been there since the 1980s, and I was only there for a month, so I cannot speak to how Japan is today, but my experience with 1980s Japan was deeply affecting.

Every culture and every time period shape its people. You might say we are discipled by our culture and times, just as we are discipled by Jesus. Sometimes this discipleship is a competition, as when the values of the culture compete with the values of God's kingdom. Other times we see the values line up.

Why do we forget this when we open our Bibles? Because the Bible is the inspired word of God with unchanging truth, we do not factor in the cultural contrasts between our times and theirs. When we read the Bible, we often do not consider how the passages translate into our unique challenges today; we just adopt them wholesale as something we should do and be.

I am particularly thinking of Paul and his magnificent statement, "To live is Christ and to die is gain" (Philippians 1:21). What a statement! He was saying something simple and profound: "As long as I am alive, I will live for Christ, but with all the suffering and hardship I endure, I would prefer death sooner rather than later. That would be a gain for me." When you look at what Paul faced, you can imagine the relief he felt in anticipating his earthly death, hoping it would come quickly so he could live eternally in the "no more tears, no more suffering" place, face-to-face with his Lord and friend. Paul lived in a severe culture and faced unending physical and mental anguish from his previous religious friends. He paid an immense price for converting to Christianity.

When our lives are touched by predominantly physical and emotional suffering, as Paul's life was, we long for heaven. We want to be with God now. If we think about some classic hymns and worship songs, the ones that speak of heaven the most or the ones that point to Jesus rescuing us from this earth were written during cultural oppression and suffering. "Swing low, sweet chariot," sang the slaves on those horrific chain gangs, "coming for to carry me home." Come quickly, Lord Jesus.

How many times in your life have you prayed, "Come quickly, Lord Jesus"? I have prayed it a few dozen times or more, usually during intense grief over a loved one or after another school shooting. But it is not a daily prayer of mine. Most days, I like life on this earth.

That is because I live with a goal that is the opposite of Paul's. I don't want a short life; I want the longest life possible. Here would be my honest prayer: "Lord, let me live a long and comfortable life. Let me watch my grandchildren walk down the aisle in marriage. After that, Lord, let me be with you for eternity. That would indeed be sweet relief." My prayer is a reflection of the culture in which I am formed.

Paul says, "To live is Christ and to die is gain." For me, to live is gain, and to die is Christ.

When earthly life looks better than the afterlife, then "to live is gain." When the afterlife looks better than earthly life, then "to die is gain."

What are we to do about this? It is a complex and nuanced situation because there is nothing wrong with wanting a long and fruitful life, but we see our value and Paul's value in stark contrast. I have pointed out several times that I think it is futile to try to be more like Paul because it simply doesn't work to transplant him out of his time and place and into ours.

CULTURAL FORCES AND THE GOSPEL

How do we live faithfully for Jesus while being formed and forged by our unique times? The answer is not feeling guilty that we feel differently than Paul, and it is not trying to be more like him. I have found it most helpful to become aware of the forces at work that drive and compel me, the unique challenges of discipleship in my own time and place. These conversations are complex and best done in community. For most people from majority culture, we have much to discuss because we live in a culture that reinforces "self" so strongly. Paul and the New Testament followers of Jesus lived in a culture that oppressed and killed them. Some cultures of oppression actually forge our discipleship, but cultures of freedom and indulgence compete with the gospel.

As you consider the culture in which you live and the forces that forge you, what cultural forces and values run counter to the gospel? I live in the United States. Four core values where I live are freedom, personal rights, safety, and wealth-building for security. At first, you might think American freedom is a gospel value, but it is tricky because even though it uses the same word, it means something radically different. Gospel freedom is being set free from the bondage of slavery to sin. God has broken the curse and released us from the prison of sin. God has freed us to attach to him. In contrast, American freedom means, "I am free to do whatever I want. I get to choose my destiny and life. I can define myself, and you do not get to define me." I am an immigrant to the United States, so I am aware that I may be defining a more current understanding of American freedom than one from earlier times, but as I listen to Americans talk about freedom, I think that is what they mean.

We also value personal rights in this country. This value is connected to freedom. As we study Scripture, we see that many people, including Jesus, sacrificed personal rights for the sake of their gospel. Paul was a Roman citizen, which was a rare privilege. But he never used his citizenship for personal benefit. He didn't even use it to help Christians. He used his citizenship only when it gave him an opportunity to share the gospel with a Roman official. I see so many Christians in this country who wield their personal rights against other citizens. What might it look like for us to sacrifice our personal rights for the sake of others—even for the sake of our enemies?

Safety is another a huge value where I live, but frankly, Jesus is much less concerned with my personal safety than I am. As I read about Jesus' interaction with John the Baptist, for instance, I don't see an example of someone who was overly concerned with John's health and safety. But so many of our prayers center around that topic.

Wealth can be a gift, especially when wealthy people use their resources to fuel kingdom endeavors and help people, but I find myself tempted to store and hoard wealth so I can relax. My default is to wish for 20 percent more than I have now. It is not to depend on God for my needs or to focus on storing up "treasures in heaven, where moths and vermin do not destroy" (Matthew 6:20).

Of course, the culture in which I live embodies gospel values too. Not everything in this culture pushes me away from the way of Jesus. Some of the values help foster my discipleship. I come from a Western culture like that of the United States, but Australia has very different values. When I moved to America, I was struck by two core cultural values that embody the gospel. *First, Americans are incredibly generous.* Much of my own journey in this country has been enhanced by the generosity of American Christians. The colossal amount of money and resources they put into their cities and into work around the globe is staggering. When I was growing up, Australians were much more measured and even miserly with their money.

The next cultural value has to do with success. In Australia, if someone is successful, we tend to cut them down to size. We call it the "tall poppy syndrome." Poppy fields are beautiful because as you look across a field of poppy flowers, you notice that every one of them is exactly the same size. Why? Because someone went through the field and cut down any individual flower that got too tall. But the United States has no such baggage around success. *People here are genuinely encouraging, supportive, and excited when others thrive.* This feels like a cultural value that lines up with the gospel and deploys us into service.

My point is not to dive into the comparison game but to simply invite us to reflect on the culture in which we are formed. How can we sift our cultural values through the gospel? Some of those values pull us toward Jesus, and some pull us away. How can we live as "peculiar people" (1 Peter 2:9 KJV) among our neighbors? These are difficult and ongoing conversations.

As you reflect on your culture, what are some values you think line up with the gospel:

-
-
-
-
-
-

What are some values that run counter to the gospel?

-
-
-
-
-

What are some habits and practices you can move into this month that will help you swim across the currents of your culture?

-
-
-
-
-
-

"YOU HAVE HEARD IT SAID . . ."

Once we've followed Jesus for a while, we discover that spiritual progress isn't always additive; sometimes it requires taking a step backward. We assume spiritual growth is all about learning, but unlearning is just as essential.

I am struck by how much of Jesus' discipling of his followers could be categorized as "unlearning." Jesus spent a good portion of his ministry reframing who God is and how God's kingdom operates so people could unlearn what they always thought to be true and relearn what is actually true. This approach is what caused the religious leaders to be so furious with Jesus. Unlearning can be painful and even threatening, especially when we have invested decades into thinking the other way. Especially when Jesus is violating our deepest core values about who God is. Especially when our own power structures are threatened by his teaching.

One of Jesus' recurring phrases was, "You have heard it said . . . but I say to you . . ." You have heard it said that *this is the way to connect with God*, but I say to you that *it is this way.* Much of Jesus' ministry was reframing, correcting, and teaching people so they could experience the Father as Jesus experienced the Father.

I think about a good Jewish lad like Peter and what it must have been like for him to unlearn. One of Peter's frequent responses to Jesus was, "No, Lord." Jesus would say something that utterly contradicted everything Peter thought he knew about God, and his immediate response was a big nope. I think about Peter's dream in Acts 10. Luke records that Peter was hungry and drifted into a trance in which he dreamed about food. As the food buffet was being lowered from heaven, Peter saw kosher and non-kosher food next to each other and grew very alarmed when God invited him to eat all of it. Peter had not eaten a single shrimp cocktail in his life. He had never once enjoyed turtle soup. His faith, synagogue, family, his wider community, the people he deeply respected, and the Torah all reinforced what he knew to be true about God: God's holiness is violated by what you put in your body.

But God had a new word for Peter: "Do not call anything impure that God has made clean" (Acts 10:15). Thus God sent Peter on a rapid and remarkable journey of unlearning. Before he knew it, Peter was chatting with a Gentile, unlearning out loud in real time. Peter told Cornelius and the relatives and friends who had gathered, "You are well aware that it is against our law for a Jew to associate with or visit a Gentile. But God has shown me that I should not call anyone impure or unclean" (verse 28). I wonder what it was like for Cornelius to receive Peter and then sit through Peter saying, "I am really not comfortable being with you, but God said I need to." It all worked out in the end, with Cornelius and his entire household becoming believers in Jesus.

I speak with so many people whose childhood experience of the church was complex. For some it was wonderful. They were known and loved. For others it was terrifying, built on a fear of hellfire or a fear of displeasing God, which was the worst thing imaginable. The adults in those churches were good people, salt of the earth in many ways, but they were perpetuating the fear they had been taught as kids. I am haunted by what the kids in our churches will need to unlearn when the time comes. We preach "grace, grace, grace," but is it possible in their black-and-white brains that they heard "fear" and will have their own unraveling journey? I pray I will welcome it and not be defensive. Unlearning can be a path of freedom for all of us.

I don't know how to unlearn on my own. I only know how to do it in community. I find it so helpful to speak openly about what I am learning and unlearning, building and deconstructing. I encourage you to bring your unlearning into your community too.

For most, unlearning is complex and slow work. I have found it helpful to give thanks for the good and sift the inaccurate. I have also found it helpful to realize the adults in my life were likely under the same burden I was and that I am possibly passing on learnings that will need to be unraveled too. For some, what you learned needs to be burned to the ground—too much hatred or fear or judgment, not enough mercy and love.

Are you on an unlearning journey now? Here are some questions to help you work through this healthy process toward spiritual growth.

Something I am currently unlearning:

____

____

____

The most difficult part of the unlearning process is:

____

____

____

What I used to believe about God or God's character:

____

____

____

My new belief about God:

____

____

____

REDEMPTIVE OR PREVENTATIVE?

We have tackled *a lot* of assumptions in these two chapters, but we have only just begun. Discipleship is a lifelong journey of noticing and then bringing our assumptions to Jesus, asking him to sift what is true so we can focus on whatever is noble and right. Here's one last assumption that gets to the heart of the way we understand spiritual progress.

When you think about the gospel, do you think it is primarily redemptive or preventative in nature? Does the gospel primarily rescue us from trouble, or does it primarily stop us from getting into trouble?

A redemptive gospel says, "No matter what we've done and what has been done to us, we can always come home." Forgiveness, restoration, repentance, second chance, a new creation. A redemptive gospel focuses on God's unconditional and specific love for *each human being*. God makes the first move, always toward us. This gospel focuses primarily on God's love for us.

A preventative gospel says, "Live within these guidelines to honor God and express your love for God. As a side benefit, you will avoid a world of pain and heartache." Its goal is a life relatively free of regret and relational damage, a life based on a series of habits and decisions oriented around God's ways—faithfulness, obedience, worship, wisdom in choosing friendships, generosity, let our yes be yes and our no be no, build our houses on the rock so we withstand the storm. The preventative gospel focuses on us moving toward God and our love for God.

There is no question that the gospel of Jesus is both redemptive and preventative, but which do you think is primary? In the game of "Would You Rather?" we are forced to choose between two difficult options. If you were forced to choose only one dynamic of the gospel, which would you choose?

I think most of us would choose the gospel of redemption as primary. To be sure, Jesus taught both dynamics, but his life arc, his teachings, and his death and resurrection bend strongly toward the redemptive as the foundational reality of the gospel.

The problem is, most of us live day-to-day as if the gospel is primarily preventative. That makes sense to me. When I think of God's redemption, my default posture is to think of it in the past tense—God redeemed me, and now I live in response to that reality by orienting my life around God's *commands*. I do not do this to curry favor with God or to earn anything. I do it to please God and because I believe God's ways are the best ways for a human to thrive with unfettered freedom. I have come to believe that all God's commands are designed for human flourishing and to access true peace. Who wants to blow their life up with secret habits? Who wants to cause relational damage to the people they love? It is better, and frankly easier, to live in God's ways and avoid all of that. We love because God first loved us (see 1 John 4:19). That is true, and it works.

But when we live primarily in view of God's preventative gospel, we create harmful consequences, especially if we have been Christians for a while. As a pastor, I have worked with many parents who want their children to love God in the same way they love God, but their language and posture are preventative, not redemptive. When parents ask for my help, they rarely say, "We really want our children to experience God's love for them." Instead they say, "We want to raise our kids to love God." It is a very good thing for your kids to love God, except for when they have never experienced God's love first and primarily.

If we try to love God before we experience God's love, we are in danger of practicing legalism, getting on the more-of-the-same and try-harder treadmills, and that can be soul-sucking. Other religions teach us to love God, but the Christian gospel teaches that "God loves us." It is first and foundational. We love God because God first loved us. After a while, we keep that love in the rearview mirror, and by doing so, we unintentionally communicate to those around us, including our children, that the preventative gospel is primary.

Before God's kingdom ever issued a rule, it issued an invitation. That invitation is ongoing, never-ending, and always available. God's mercies are new every morning; great is God's faithfulness (see Lamentations 3:23). God's love first. God's love always. God's faithfulness as primary. Our love for God pours out in response to God's love for us. God's love is scandalous to humans. Rich Mullins calls it a "reckless" love in his song "The Love of God."

Humans will always default to a posture in which we are at the center of everything, and it can cause us to cast ourselves as the primary actor in our own life. But the gospel of Jesus is that God acts first, and we react, not once but always. God makes the first move, and we respond. Unfortunately, over time, we tend to think our faith originates from us. These dynamics are why we quickly make our way to the preventative side.

Prevention or redemption? How might your language and posture change as you raise kids or disciple others? How might it benefit your own faith to intentionally think *redemptive first and always*?

DISCUSSION QUESTIONS

1. When you made a list of what Jesus can do that you cannot do, what struck you about it?
2. In what ways does your culture both help and hinder you as you follow Jesus?
3. What momentums do you see in your culture that pull against the gospel?
4. When you are at your best, making your best kingdom contribution, what does that look like?
5. How does your kingdom contribution benefit others?
6. Do you think the gospel is first redemptive or preventative?
7. What are you unlearning right now, and how is that going?

NINE

HOME AND SHALOM

We come to God by love, not by navigation.
SAINT AUGUSTINE

"Where is home for you?"

As soon as the therapist asked Patti that question, she knew exactly what he meant. He wasn't asking the location of her house; he was asking where she went to feel completely herself, connected to God, and fully loved. Patti had reluctantly come in for therapy after realizing she couldn't process her trauma alone. She spent the first session pouring out her recent story—what happened to her, the breach of trust and subsequent flooding of emotions she couldn't contain and behaviors she couldn't manage. The therapist had discerned that Patti was living in hypervigilance. She struggled to let her guard down and relax. The wounds had made her cagey, wary of even the people closest to her.

She described where home was for her, and her answer was very concrete. She knew the place, the things she would be doing, and those she would be with to be truly "home."

His next question was an invitation: "When was the last time you went home?"

It had been a long time. Like many of us, Patti was caught up in all she had to do and had not carved out time to go "home." Her vocation was based around serving people, and like many of us in serving vocations, she felt selfish when she took care of herself. She kept pushing, pushing, pushing to the point of exhaustion. As the session wrapped up, her therapist gave her "home" work. "I'd like you to go home before our next session and then come back and tell me how it went." He was inviting her to take the necessary time to connect and heal so she could be well and thriving again.

Patti took her therapist seriously and scheduled time to go "home." At her next session, she walked into his office, and her therapist said, "Ah, I see you've been home." He could tell a difference just in her countenance and posture.

We could all use more "home" work in our lives.

SHALOM AND SELF-RIGHTEOUSNESS

Home is anywhere we are fully welcomed and accepted, free to love and be loved. Our guard is down; we do not need to strive; we do not need to be anything more than we are; and we are well. We are well with God, well with ourselves, well with our people. We are rejuvenated, breathing easy, and thriving. But we are not just receiving. Our hearts are opened up to freely give to others.

Home is not necessarily comfort, nor is it safe, but it is always belonging, always encountering love. Home is where we experience God's profound and specific love for us. We are able to relax into it and then generously pour it out to others, including marginalized people and enemies. Going home is what allows us to risk, explore, and sacrifice for the needs of others.

If this is home, then the Hebrew Scriptures word for it is *shalom*. The word *shalom* makes most of us think of a greeting or "peace." That is a fine start, but *shalom* goes much deeper than our modern understanding of peace. It has more to do with human flourishing than simply a peaceful existence. When we translate words from one culture to another, they can lose some horsepower. *Shalom* is like a vocabulary superfood that is packed with all manner of meaning and power.

Shalom means "thriving," "wholeness," " well-being." Shalom is not measured simply through individual wellness; the wellness of an entire community is in view here. True shalom involves every relationship in a society—with ourselves, God, our people, strangers, the under-resourced, enemies, immigrants, creation, all of it. All people are well, not just the well-off and well-to-do.

How do we know when we are well? One of the simplest ways is to learn what it feels like to be connected. When we are unwell, we disconnect from ourselves; we are no longer aware of what is going on in us. We disconnect from God and from people. We see people as an enemy or someone we don't care about. We either don't think about God or we see God as "watching us from a distance," as that '80s Bette Midler song used to say. When we sense that we are disconnected, we can pause and find our way home.

As I seek to be home with God and as I seek shalom, I have to learn a new discipline. I tend to ask God to remove things so I or a loved one can get shalom. I confess that my default prayer is some version of, "Lord, please remove ___________ from my life," or "please remove ___________ from my loved one's life." "Lord, please remove cancer. Please remove this or that obstacle." Even after all these years, my default belief is that peace and well-being come from absence, so I often ask God to take something away—conflict, disease, difficult or evil people.

But the peace of Christ more often infects our situation as it is rather than removing the situation. I have known this truth for decades, but I've been slow to learn it. Or maybe I am slow to be okay with it. I know it for a season, or I see a glimpse of it, but then my default posture switches back to "God, take this away."

I try to reorient around the way shalom works by intentionally practicing relaxing into God's presence. I first learned this when I was a hospital chaplain—mostly out of survival. The onslaught of death, trauma, cancer diagnoses, and general suffering overwhelmed me, and I was drowning in all that was going on inside of me. I couldn't manage myself or the pressure to say the right thing or do the right thing, but I desperately wanted to be helpful to people in the worst moments of their lives. This was the crucible where I first started looking for God's peace in the midst of suffering and death.

My anxiety said I had to figure it out; I had to know what to say; it was all on me; and my job was to make everything better. When I learned to notice those triggers, I could pause, get off the anxiety treadmill, remember that God was with me and ahead of me with the suffering family, and relax into God's presence. It turns out, we can experience home and shalom anywhere.

Yet that early chaplaincy experience did not forge a lifelong habit for me. I still need to relearn how to practice shalom. I keep defaulting back to "shalom means God takes it away," or "find shalom in my own strength."

Another way to say "relax into God's presence" might be "trust God's righteousness over my own." The word *righteousness* appears throughout the New Testament, but we often limit its meaning to what Jesus did on the cross. I find it much more helpful to consider righteousness in my daily reality, not just in a past event. *Righteousness* is "New Testament shalom," so when I read about righteousness in Scripture, I think "wellness." Where do I look for my righteousness? What do I depend on to be well?

When I forget the Lord, I have moved into a *self*-righteousness. Self-righteousness can come across as if I think I am better than others, which is perhaps the most common understanding of it. But as we discussed in chapter 5, some self-righteous people go the other way. They are full of themselves, but their self-righteousness is expressed through either self-pity or self-condemnation. They don't think too highly of themselves; they think too lowly. But they still depend on their self for what is true and right. Arrogance can certainly be self-righteousness, but so can insecurity. As we explored when we looked into our inner critics, many of us struggle to relax into God because we believe ourselves over God. That is a form of well-meaning self-righteousness. We cannot be in shalom when we depend on self.

This is why I advocate for putting ourselves on our conscious list of relationships. If we don't, then we are strangers to ourselves; we are disconnected. We are not in shalom. We are far from home. When we pay attention to ourselves in the sort of work I am advocating for in this book, we get to know ourselves and discover the parts of ourselves that depend on self instead of God.

When I first took seriously what was going on in myself, I was shocked to discover just how much self-righteousness I carried on any given day. I depended on self a lot, sometimes through high insecurity, sometimes through high arrogance, but always with self at the forefront. I was both alarmed and excited to discover all this self-reliance, as it gave me a lot to repent of, but it also meant I had a lot of room for more freedom in my life. As Christians, it's alarming to discover just how often we rely on ourselves to be well rather than folding our lives into Christ. When we depend on self, we are bound; when we depend on God, we are free. When we repent of that self-reliance, we relax into God's presence, which enables us to viscerally experience the presence, love, and freedom of Christ that is available to us.

I became excited to repent because repentance leads to truth and freedom. In fact, I did so much repenting in those early days that it became a new hobby. I repented in my spare time. I repented recreationally. I have a few core hobbies—craft coffee, good guitars, fly-fishing, and repentance.

The call to repent in Scripture is an invitation to shalom, to be well. It is a call to turn from self and to fold into the righteousness of God. We no longer operate under our own steam. We no longer determine what is right and true. We trust that God is right and true, and we intentionally believe God over ourselves.

SIN AS A NOUN

What about sin? Sin is tricky to talk about because our minds quickly move to a list of things we should and should not do. When we think *sin,* we think *morality* or *right and wrong.* Sin is a moral topic, to be sure, but the authors of Scripture see sin more as a breach than a list, more as a dire severance than ethical commands. They talk about sin more as a condition we are in than as the specific things we do or do not do. I particularly appreciate the way Paul talks about sin in the New Testament, especially in his letter to the Romans, because he describes it much more as a noun than he does as a verb. For Paul, sin is something we're in more than something we do. Paul uses high alarm and warning language to help us stay out of sin's grip. In Romans 6, Paul uses stark language to call us to protect ourselves from sin because sin entraps us and then punishes us without mercy. Paul says that if we're not careful, we will fall into the grip of sin. It will squeeze the very life out of us. Sin kills and destroys.

In contrast to sin, God gives life. Paul says that whatever we give ourselves to—sin or God—will consume us. So if we hand ourselves over to sin, then sin will be the dominant controller of our lives. If we've met someone who has depended on self for a long time, we have seen this play out in a tragic way. They may not be drug-addicted or homeless and living on the street, but they have spent decades depending on self to be well. No one can ever tell them anything because they always know better than anyone else does. They cannot open up their heart to trust or vulnerability because they can only depend on self to be safe. They cannot receive a compliment because their inner critic has them in a death grip. When they do relational damage, they have to ignore it. They find it difficult to say, "I was wrong." This is the tragic and destructive power of sin, and God offers to rescue us from it.

Our modern misunderstanding is that God punishes us when we sin. But many of the Scripture writers point out that sin punishes us when we sin. God warns us not to fall into the lure of sin because it will turn on us and make us pay. Though we imagine that God enjoys punishing us when we sin, that is not true. When a mother warns her child not to touch a hot stove and then the child touches the stove and gets burned, the mother doesn't say, "Actually, I was hoping you would do that so I could punish you." More likely, the mother rushes in alarmed. "That's why I told you not to do it! Let me take care of that burn." The stove, not the mother, did the punishing.

A few years ago, I stumbled across the writings of a Catholic priest named Herbert McCabe, and the way he talked about sin stopped me in my tracks. McCabe suggested that the reason to avoid sin is that it pollutes our thinking. Sin makes us think that God has changed God's view of us. But McCabe proposed that sin doesn't change God's view of us; sin changes *our view of God's view of us*. Sin infects and distorts our capacity to see God for who God really is. So when we sin, we no longer see God as a loving Father; we see God as a judge or a harsh taskmaster.

McCabe writes these words in his book *Faith within Reason*:

> Take the famous parable of the prodigal son (Lk. 15:11–32). In this, the younger son goes to a distant country far from his father and squanders all his father's gifts in debauchery and generally having a high old time. After a bit he sees himself for what he is, so as to say, "I am no longer worthy to be called your son; treat me as one of your hired servants." What his sin has done is to alter his whole relationship with his father; instead of being a son he now should be treated as one who gets his *wages*, gets exactly what he deserves. But there are two things here; there is the fact that this is what his

> sin has *done*, and there is the fact that he *recognizes* this. To make sure you see that this is the crucial point of the story, Luke has it repeated twice. The vital thing is that the son has recognized his sin for what it is: something that changes God into a paymaster, or a judge. Sin is something that changes God into a projection of our guilt, so that we don't see the real God at all; all we see is some kind of judge. God (the whole meaning and purpose and point of our existence) has become a condemnation of us. God has been turned into Satan, the accuser of man, the paymaster, the one who weighs our deeds and condemns us.[1]

I am fascinated by this. As I read the parable of the prodigal son in Luke 15, I notice the older brother's distortion. We see that the father never changed, nor did his posture change toward either of his sons. Instead, their view of his posture changed. That is what sin does. It infects us and puts us in a false reality. Repentance, then, is stepping out of sin's grip or out of self-righteousness and remembering that our righteousness and well-being are found in the life-giver, not the death squeeze of sin and self. Repentance increases our chances of encountering God for who God really is.

In his book *Orthodoxy*, G. K. Chesterton claims that sin ages us. He writes about God's absolute wonder and enjoyment of creation. He imagines that God handcrafts every flower and commands every sunset. God is a creator, so nothing is automated. And God never tires of all this creative energy, even though God is doing the same thing again and again every day, and every day exults in it. Chesterton says God must be playful like a child because a child never tires of repetition. When we toss a child in the air, the child says, "Do it again!" Our arms wear out way before the child's interest wears out. Chesterton provokes our thinking, suggesting that God is better at being a kid than we are. God does not grow old, weary, or bored.

1. Herbert McCabe, *Faith within Reason* (New York: Continuum, 2007), 155–56.

Chesterton writes, "We have sinned and grown old, and our Father is younger than we."[2]

Jesus breaks the lure and effect of sin in our lives. This is the miracle of salvation. I want God to take suffering and temptation away, and I want God to make me a perfect person, but God does something more remarkable—God changes what my heart wants. I used to want sin because I was self-righteous. I needed things from people or needed to do things to and for people so I could be "well" with myself. It never worked. But when I relaxed into God's presence, I was able to fold my life into God's righteousness and experience true, everlasting wellness.

The more I experience God's shalom, the less appeal sin has. God has changed my heart's desire. I can still very much fall into temptation because I am human, but I find that if I can relax into God's presence, I can clearly see both paths: God's path of life and sin's path of death. My goal—and I hit this goal some of the time and miss it much of the time—is to let God's first and last word overrule all my incessant words. I want to live into God's first and last word so my reality is formed by God's truth and my incessant chatter doesn't stand a chance.

That sounds like home to me. That is full-body shalom.

RESERVOIR OR CANAL?

One reason to be well or seek shalom is because it naturally benefits others. Just as chronic anxiety is infectious, so is shalom. When a few are well, the many can become well. When people are in shalom, others want to be around them. They have something that others want. Jesus is the ultimate embodiment of shalom, which is why he was so captivating to those who were hungering to be well.

2. G. K. Chesterton, *Orthodoxy* (New York: Lane, 1909), 109.

The end of all this work is not us; it is God and God's mission to serve and redeem others. The purpose of every human is to worship our creator, and our mission is to further God's kingdom. We share this good news with those who are not yet worshiping, those who have not yet oriented their lives around God but are oriented around self. This work frees us to serve in even the most difficult human circumstances. It allows us to move into places of evil and great suffering and work for justice and mercy.

This world breaks people, and many among us need solidarity, advocacy, and love. Systems and structures in this world can be harsh and exploitive, and our imperative is to bring shalom to everyone, not just keep it for ourselves. When we are well with God, we are free to give and serve sacrificially. Church history bears witness to those who served by pouring out their lives on behalf of others.

But even as we do, we must heed this warning from Bernard of Clairvaux:

> The man who is wise, therefore, will see his life as more like a reservoir than a canal. The canal simultaneously pours out what it receives; the reservoir retains the water till it is filled, then discharges the overflow without loss to itself. . . . You too must learn to await this fullness before pouring out your gifts, do not try to be more generous than God.[3]

I am challenged by Bernard's startling warning: "Do not try to be more generous than God." It is a reminder that God gives and loves out of the overflow, yet I tend to pour it all out in the name of God, getting anxious and weary as I go. When I intentionally let God fill me and serve out of that abundance, I am well. More reservoir, less canal. It is a challenge I struggle to maintain.

---

3. Bernard of Clairvaux, "Sermon 18, 'The Two Operations of the Holy Spirit,'" in *The Works of Bernard of Clairvaux: On The Song of Songs I* (Kalamazoo, MI: Cistercian, 1977), 134, 136.

One reason I love the Life-Giving List tool I described in the previous chapter is that it forces me to receive from God rather than always focusing on others to pour into. As you consider living out of the overflow rather than pouring everything out, go on a specific hunt for the love of God this month. What might your life look like if you stubbed your toe on the goodness of God several times this month? How might that free you to connect with and serve others?

OFF THE HOOK

Sometimes when I am teaching the tools and approaches covered in this book, someone will say, "It feels like you are letting us off the hook." I take this as a very positive statement, but they say it with alarm, as though being let off the hook is a dangerous thing. If we are not on the hook, will we become complacent and self-absorbed? It really is stunning to consider just how much humans are motivated by fear instead of love. In response, I gently ask, "What hook are you on? What kind of God would put you on a hook?" Not the God of the Bible. The God of the Bible sacrificed God's one and only Son so we would never have to be on a hook again. Jesus was crucified on a literal hook so we could be set free. Perfect love casts out fear, and we need not worry about a hook or a God who is looking to hang us on a hook. In the person and work of Jesus Christ, all of that was taken care of. I can be free of fear, thanks to Christ, and can encounter God's love and shalom with no worry about being skewered.

Do you want to be well? Do you want to embody freedom and the love of God and let those realities animate you to serve others? I pray the tools and approaches in this book can help you connect deeply to God, to others, and to yourself. My experience has been that these tools are not something we do and then graduate from but that they become habits that help us navigate life. They take intentionality and courage at first, but over time, they move to the back of our brains as we practice relaxing into God's presence, learn to trust God's word over our own, identify our false needs, and get off the comparison treadmill. Be kind to yourself as you continue on this journey, and may the peace of Christ be with you.

DISCUSSION QUESTIONS

1. Where is home for you?
2. What "home" work might you try this week to experience home?
3. When you think of the word *sin*, what primarily comes to mind?
4. What do you think of Herbert McCabe's notion that "sin distorts our view of God's view of us?"
5. When do you feel most fully and completely loved?
6. What life-giving habits will you cultivate in the next thirty days?
7. What might it look like to try to be "more generous than God"? What might you do this week to serve out of the overflow rather than pour everything out?

ACKNOWLEDGMENTS

Thanks to—

- My Zondervan team, especially Kyle Rohane, Alexis de Weese, and Dirk Buursma. You have gone above and beyond in supporting and caring for me in one of the most intense seasons of my life. Thank you for your belief in me and your great care in helping this project come to fruition. Thank you for the Zoom calls, the feedback, and the careful nurturing of this project. It is a far superior offering because of your guidance.
- My agent Don Pape. You quickly became a trusted friend and a force of encouragement in my life. Thank you for advocating for this work, praying for me, cheering me on, and challenging me. Also, I love how much you love books!
- The Discovery Church congregation. What a privilege to serve as your pastor for sixteen years. You are the community that helped forge and refine my faith and let me field-test many of these thoughts and tools.
- My sister, Toni, who first introduced me to Jesus Christ. You continue to inspire me by your fierce dedication and advocacy and just plain old-fashioned fun. You are a first-class aunt to my kids and sister to Lisa and me.

- My children Bryson, Andrew, and Kaylee. I hit the jackpot when I got to be your dad. I am so grateful to get an up-close view of your amazing lives. You each face this world in a way that inspires and teaches me. I am so proud of who you are and how you are in this world.
- My wife, Lisa. You are a healer, and God has healed much in me through who you are. The fact that I get to bear witness to your life is sometimes more than I can contain. You are phenomenal to me.
- My King, Jesus Christ, who redeemed a lost and confused young boy and in whom I live and move and have my being with great delight and relish.

APPENDIX 1

ADDITIONAL RESOURCES

Below are some resources for further exploration.

TRADITIONAL SYSTEMS THEORY

Friedman, Edwin H. *Friedman's Fables*. New York: Guilford Press, 1990.

This book contains a wonderfully and playfully provocative set of fables to illustrate various systems approaches.

Gilbert, Roberta M. *The Eight Concepts of Bowen Theory*. Lake Frederick, VA: Leading Systems Press, 2004.

Gilbert gives a solid overview of the core concepts that Murray Bowen postulated.

MODERN ADAPTATIONS OF SYSTEMS THEORY

Herrington, Jim, Trisha Taylor, and R. Robert Creech. *The Leader's Journey*. Second edition. Grand Rapids: Baker Academic, 2020.

The Leader's Journey is a classic on systems in Christian leadership.

Smith, Kathleen. *Everything Isn't Terrible*. New York: Hachette, 2019.

Smith, a therapist in Washington, D.C., writes brilliantly and comically about systems in her clients.

Watzlawick, Paul, John H. Weakland, and Richard Fisch. *Change: Principles of Problem Formation and Problem Resolution*. New York: Norton, 2011.

The authors give a deep and technical dive into stuck patterns and attempted solutions.

SPIRITUAL GROWTH AND HEALTH

Collier, Winn. *A Burning in My Bones: The Authorized Biography of Eugene H. Peterson*. Colorado Springs: WaterBrook, 2021.

A Burning in My Bones is an utterly beautifully written account of a pastor who relaxed into God's presence.

Ortberg, John. *The Life You've Always Wanted*. Grand Rapids: Zondervan, 2002.

This book remains a classic for a reason. Ortberg makes following Jesus accessible and tangible.

Villodas, Rich. *The Deeply Formed Life*. Colorado Springs: WaterBrook, 2020.

Villodas uses systems theory as a lens for spiritual formation. His approach is holistic, kind, and brilliant.

APPENDIX 2

GAUNTLET QUESTIONS

I have hosted a podcast since 2018, and when I interview guests, one of the distinctive features has been the "gauntlet of anxiety" questions. For most guests, I ask three to five questions. Over the years, I have collected a number of questions (see below for a master list of all the questions). Using these questions is helpful to get to know someone, as well as the world's worst party icebreakers!

Gauntlet

1. How do you know when you are not well?
2. What practice—that takes five minutes or less—helps you connect with God?
3. What sort of leadership situations generate anxiety for you?
4. What types of people trigger you the most?
5. What do you do to stay connected to them?
6. Sometimes we can be the last to know when we're not okay. Who in your life knows before you know?
7. When you think about your family of origin, what is one asset and one liability that you've inherited from them?
8. In the absence of information, people connect the dots in the most pathological way possible. What goes through your mind when you're anxious but don't have all the information?

9. In your leadership, where do you keep running into yourself? What trait do you wish you could break?
10. Criticism is tough. What type of criticism most affects you?
11. Cumulative criticism can take you out. Tell us about a season that felt like unrelenting criticism.
12. What if I were at least as _______ to myself as God is?
13. Where do you experience a gap between what you believe and what you experience?
14. How do you mind that gap?
15. If you treated yourself as well as you treated others, what one way of dealing with yourself would you change?
16. Can you share a time you witnessed a miracle? What happened?
17. What have you found helpful to do in order to deal with loneliness?
18. When recently have you felt free?
19. Tell us about a time in the last few weeks when you were at peace.
20. What is a habit or practice—or a person you know—that helps you relax into the presence of God?
21. When in your life do you feel most fully loved?

APPENDIX 3

THE LIFE-GIVING LIST

You can also download a digital copy at www.stevecusswords.com/resources. I also feature the Life-Giving List in a twelve-week journal available on that site for those who want to dig deeper.

Most of us are prone to neglect our own well-being. When we get reactive, we lose our imagination and get stuck in binary thinking. But God has given us many gifts we can enjoy, and participating in these gifts helps us relax into God's presence. I encourage you to take a month and pay attention to God's particular gifts to you and add them to the list.

Make sure each column has a range of options—from activities that take a few minutes to several days, from pursuits that cost nothing to those that cost a lot. The secret to this list is threefold: getting concrete about what life gives you, intentionally calendaring your planning of activities, and thanking and worshiping God as you participate in anything on this list.

What has God given that you love? Nothing is too trivial or too extravagant. Go ahead and make your list.

PEOPLE	REMOTE OR LOCAL?	PLACES

COST AND TIME	ACTIVITIES	COST AND TIME